LIVING IN THE PRESENCE

LIVING
IN THE
PRESENCE

*Spiritual Exercises to Open Your Life
to the Awareness of God*

Tilden Edwards

HarperSanFrancisco
A Division of HarperCollins*Publishers*

Acknowledgment is made for the Haiku poem by Ken Feit reprinted from "The Little Magazine" by permission of Bear & Company, Inc., Santa Fe, New Mexico.

Unless otherwise noted, Scripture quotations contained herein are from the Revised Standard Version of the Bible, copyrighted 1946, 1952, 1971 by the Division of Christian Education of the National Council of Churches of Christ in the U.S.A., and are used by permission. All rights reserved. Other Bible translations quoted are the Jerusalem Bible (JB) and the New American Bible (NAB).

FIRST HARPERCOLLINS PAPERBACK EDITION PUBLISHED IN 1994

Library of Congress Cataloging-in-Publication Data

Edwards, Tilden.
    Living in the presence : spiritual exercises to open your life to
the awareness of God / Tilden Edwards. — 1st HarperCollins pbk. ed.
      p.   cm.
    Includes bibliographical references.
    ISBN 0–06–062127–3 (pbk. : alk paper)
    1. Spiritual life—Christianity.   2. Spiritual exercises.
I. Title.
BV4501.2.E3173   1995
248.3—dc20   94–24965
                                          CIP

98 HAD 10 9 8 7

For Mary,
my dearly beloved and steady
companion in the Presence

Contents

Acknowledgments

I am particularly indebted to Gerald May and Jeannette Bakke for their very perceptive and detailed critique of my manuscript. I am also thankful to other Shalem staff members and spiritual guidance program graduates who have helpfully reviewed particular sections of it: Marlene Maier, Rose Mary Dougherty, Isabella Bates, Lindsley Ludy, Cecilia Braveboy, Eileen Colbert, John Becker, Barbara Osborne, and Joan Nesser. Father Thomas Keating, O.C.S.O., was especially helpful in critiquing my interpretation of Centering Prayer, as well as the introductory discussion of spiritual identity. Bruce Rigdon provided helpful comments on icons. Though he did not see the manuscript, I am indebted to the Venerable Tarthang Tulku for his many challenging insights over the years regarding contemplative awareness and practice.

I want to offer my gratitude to those hundreds of people in long-term groups of the Shalem Institute with whom I have had the privilege of seeing God's abundant grace at work, and who have shared and tested with me some form of most of the prayer exercises in this book.

I am also thankful to those who helped assure quiet space for the most intensive part of the writing: Victoria Jenez and the Vallombrosa Center in Menlo Park, California, and Thomas McCusker, who graciously loaned me his cabin in West Virginia.

List of Exercises

The prayer exercises in this book are adaptable for both groups and individuals. They need not be done in the sequence in which they occur in the book. Some are more subtle or delicate than others and may best be undertaken later by those who are less experienced in quiet prayer, especially exercises 8 and 9 (which you may want to skip entirely), 4, and 12 through 14. However, different people, regardless of background, tend to respond quite differently to these exercises, given each person's unique, evolving relationship to God; you need to be guided by your own sense of God's invitation in deciding which exercises are appropriate at a given time. This is especially true when it comes to incorporating an exercise into your regular practice on a long-term basis. Only one or a very few of these practices may be right for assisting your ongoing, deepening presence to God at a given time. Part 2, on supporting, goes into more detail about the use of these and other exercises in groups.

The instructions guide you into different ways of intentionally being present to God and reflecting on your experience and awareness. You may find that in some cases your actual experience does not follow the particular interpretive imagery of the instructions. If so, that's fine. The imagery is meant to be suggestive for your opening to God, not prescriptive or definitive. As Dom John Chapman once said, "Pray as you can and not as you can't." The important thing is that you desire to become available to God through whatever may emerge. The instructions are strictly a means to assist this end, and you may rightly find yourself making modifications that are best for you.

The reflection questions suggested after exercise 4 with slight modification can be asked after most of the other exercises (either in addition to or in place of their accompanying reflection questions).

Once in a while special suggestions are given for "homework," i.e., daily practice after an initial experience. In most cases though, the exercise as presented can simply be repeated as you may be moved.

Introduction

In the fall of 1973 twenty people gathered together in Washington, D.C., out of many different denominational and personal backgrounds. We committed ourselves to meet weekly for at least two hours over the next ten months. We were responding to some mysterious invitation in each of us to become more attentive to the deep Wellspring of our lives. We wanted help and support for this subtle process. We did not find it adequately amongst the resources we knew.

Together we found means from different classical sources that helped our bodies, minds, and hearts become more vulnerable to the Spirit. We also discovered how difficult this process could be, how graced it often was, and how dependent it is on God's timing and our true willingness. Over the years more and more people sought us out. What we thought was perhaps an aberrant need of a few people in fact turned out to be the need of many, a need reflected in the wide-ranging spiritual awakening of our time.

That awakening at its best has been claiming both a wider and a deeper heritage of spiritual formation, bursting the normal bounds of many operational denominational practices, and yet trying to maintain and draw out the authentic spiritual depth of each heritage. The spiritual life has always overflowed human-made boundaries. That is part of its prophetic quality, drawing us toward that fuller community of faith that is beyond our separated circles.

Such realizations led to the establishment of the ecumenical Shalem Institute for Spiritual Formation and to its broad range of offerings aimed at complementing or deepening what was available in local churches, theological schools, monasteries, and retreat centers. We have special concern for the contemplative depth of Christian tradition for active people who care about radiating God's love for the world through countless vocations. This contemplative depth we have found particularly missing in normal Christian formation, to the great loss and sometimes distortion of the gospel's fullness.

CONTEMPLATIVE FORMATION

By *contemplative* I mean attention to our direct, loving, receptive, trusting presence for God. This attention includes the desire to be present through and beyond our images, thoughts, and feelings. This intimate, immediate relationship is not an esoteric one meant for the few. It is our deepest human home and calling; all other homes and callings derive their authenticity from it. "A contemplative then is not a special kind of person; every person is a special kind of contemplative."[1]

This book grows out of my years of personal and corporate experience at Shalem, trying to assist an authentic spiritual formation process for people as they seem ready, with respect for their many differences. When I say *spiritual formation* I am restricting it to formation in selected disciplines and attitudes of direct attention to God—particular ways evolved through the tradition that can help us directly notice and yield to God's loving Presence as it is offered. *Spiritual formation* more broadly refers to all those mysterious ways that God seeks to form us in God's likeness through all dimensions of our individual and corporate lives.

More specifically, I have sought to take the reader through a number of dimensions of human living, looking at the ways each of them can be an arena of attentiveness to God and our true identity in God. With each dimension I have suggested exercises that might be helpful experiential practices for individuals and/or spiritual formation groups. Most of these exercises have been used in some form within Shalem groups. They are not meant to be taken as frozen forms. They need to be prayerfully adapted to your situation and continue to evolve in their ways of assisting your spiritual awareness.

I have also included chapters on the leadership of such groups, complementing an earlier work by my colleague Gerald May and a chapter on groups in one of my previous books.[2] We have found very little written in detail on the qualities of leadership needed for serious spiritual formation groups, especially ones with a contemplative emphasis. My hope is that these sections will encourage more such leadership, and that the book can be used as a text for assisting the leaders of such groups, utilizing selectively some of the exercises. I hope the book will prove equally helpful to the individual seeker. Any relevant readings will be found in the endnotes.

Please remember that this book is not intended to be a comprehensive text for contemplative spiritual formation (which I believe would be an impossible feat in any case, given the endless richness of practices and subtle personal variations of adaptation and understanding in this long tradition). It is very selective in content and emphasis, reflecting what I know best, what seems to have been helpful for others, and, in some cases, what can draw out frequently neglected or unexplored dimensions of contemplative awareness.

In the style of the book I have tried to take seriously St. Paul's admonition to "teach spiritual things spiritually . . . not in the way in which philosophy is taught" (1 Cor. 2:13, JB). In other words, I have tried to avoid a great deal of information and analysis; instead I have attempted to succinctly speak spirit to spirit, hoping to evoke the reader's own obscure firsthand awareness about the soul's realities that are always deeper than any words about them. Such a style I believe is fundamental to spiritual formation and sets it off from more objective catechesis (i.e., religious education about the Christian life). It will be a great day when it becomes standard for these two to be carefully interwoven in the larger Christian formation process.

DIFFERENT DIMENSIONS OF OUR SPIRITUAL IDENTITY

As I was writing this book I found myself returning again and again to the subject of who we are in our different modes of relationship to God. I use a variety of phrases to describe these modes of presence. An understanding of our spiritual identity is so basic to understanding the spiritual life that I will try to give a synopsis here, in the hope that it will help your clarity as you encounter this repeated emphasis. If you find it too succinct for clarity, though, don't be concerned. I hope the meanings will become more clear as they are used in the concrete contexts of your daily experience as the book goes along (to the extent that such subtle realities are capable of clarity). Please keep in mind that this is just one way spiritual identity could be described, and I include only a few selected dimensions of it.

We live with a continuum of identities in relation to God, ranging from the most separated to the most united. The lifetime process of spiritual conversion involves God's slow purging of our sense of separatedness and illumining of our true nature on the way to union with God and with God's loving will in the world.

THE FALSE SELF

In our most separated identity, we believe that an isolating, self-established sense of self is ultimate, "the real me." The result is a life lived protecting and asserting this sense of self at all costs. The self is a kind of idol that we worship; the center of the universe. If God is admitted to be a reality, in our narcissistic focus God is used to sustain and enhance this sense of "I", and all its ways.

We may expand this identity to include others like us, but the end is essentially the same. When others are included we might describe our goal like this: to sustain and enhance the security and power of the collective self through rigidly enforced ideological conformity and actions. If God is part of this collective ego, God's job is to secure and advance the group's way. If I die in defense of this way, I believe God will reward me in the next life, since I have identified God's way with this collective way.

The Crusades and current versions of religious fanaticism often include such an identity. The group and its way is not a humble transparency for the wondrous mystery of God; it is ultimately a self-securing *substitute* for God, however often God's name may be invoked. There is no experience or trust of God as being other than the one who can reflect our possessive and static sense of ego self. Charity may be affirmed, but only insofar as it satisfies the aims of the individual or collective ego that is the ultimate attachment.

WILLING-FOR-LOVE SELF

Our false identity is challenged by some other force in and around us, which in faith we call God. The challenge comes in the form of some experience of mercy, of unmerited love, that cuts through our fearful, willful ego identity. This may come through another person, or seem to come directly from God. At a more remote level this awareness of unconditional love may dawn on us through our own loves. We find ourselves intrinsically caring for someone else rather than just as someone who can meet our ego needs. Or we find ourselves unexpectedly sacrificing our time for a project that is helping people in some way.

Through such ways our identity begins to shift. Our self-centeredness is loosened, or "off-centered." We still retain a strong sense of a separate self, but loving and more open divine and human relationships are included as part of who we are. The self is more free for altruism, for the less calculating use of its gifts for God and people. We also become more capable of *appreciating* life and what is given, not just as opportunities for self-aggrandizement or fixing things up, but simply as an unpossessive end in itself.

Our most separate identity, described at the beginning of this section, I variously label as our false, fallen, possessive, or confused self. I also might refer to it as our ego self-image, little self, or constricted ego in a *willful* sense. The second level of identity, just described, I variously label our ego self-image, little self, or constricted ego in a more *neutral* or *willing-for-God* sense. As we are more graced, this becomes evermore an expedient rather than substantive sense of self: a sense of practical ego functions that are willingly available to God and neighbor and appreciative presence, while our true self is found in our relationship with God.

As long as some substantive sense of identity separate from God remains, we will retain a subject-object sense of the relationship: God is ultimately other not only than my conditioned, created ego, but ultimately other than, not part of, my essential identity. However, personal orientation increasingly is toward the God rather than the self side of the relationship. I refer to this identity when God's Spirit is in the ascendency as our big or full self identity in God; our deeper self grounded in God, which is evolving in a faith knowledge that is beyond an exclusively cognitive or sense-related knowledge. Here is the visible beginning of the new self in Christ described by St. Paul in Romans 6 and Colossians 3:9–11.

CONTEMPLATIVE AWARENESS

The third point on this continuum of spiritual identity brings us to contemplative awareness: times when our imaged sense of self is not present. This occurs naturally "between" our thoughts. For example, if we are looking at a tree, in the instant before our reflective self appears to make some commentary on the tree, we are in a sense present "in" the tree. No observer has risen to separate us "out." Such coinherence is always part of our reality, though we may not be conditioned to attend or value it. We might experience this awareness briefly at any time in our lives. This natural contemplative awareness can help us to understand the theologically described unity in diversity of the Holy Trinity, which is reflected in us, since we are made in God's image (Gen. 1:27).

With the impetus of further grace (God's free, gifted movement in and among us), met with our consent, this unity with creation is deepened to its source in God.[3] Our being in God is manifest. Our imaged substantive sense of self dissolves, and along with it our imaged sense of God. No longer is it a subject-object relationship with God, but a subject-subject relationship, so intimate and consuming as to "know" no distinction (even though in reality a distinction remains). Now we become clear that contemplation is not an experience to be gained (there is no one left to "gain" anything), but an eternal identity to be realized.[4]

In such moments we fully embody our being in God, our deepest identity in God, the true self in the heart, our deepest home and widest consciousness. We have been fully moved from the mind to the heart. We have died through Christ and into Christ, and with him share the divine Father/Mother's being. Our imaged little self can never *possess* this way of being, only relinquish itself into *participation* in it. The long process of conversion, of being turned by God's grace and our willingness from little self-centeredness to God-centeredness, finds a particular climax at this point. Here we are least conditioned by our personal and cultural experience and most directly conditioned by God. This is an embodied awareness that we will cycle in and out of for the rest of our lives. As we are "out" of it, our yearning for God grows ever deeper. As we are "in" it, we are ever more consumed by God's love.

The fallout of this process in daily life is the increasing freedom of the little self to live with a faith knowledge in its ultimate unity with the love of God in Christ and with God's creation. The fruits also include a more steady capacity to let one's reflective ego function as a truly expedient (rather than substantive, self-established) channel for that loving unity to manifest itself for the care, reconciliation, and joy of life in God. We become more capable of letting God's *shalom*, God's true peace, be shaped through and among us in a myriad of called-for ways.

The power of the false self to reassert itself never finally disappears in this life, however. It is the self that Thomas Merton says we have to "sweat out," accepting its suffering (for ourselves and caused for others), humiliation, and contradiction.[5] We need personal and collective spiritual disciplines that assist our vigilance and encourage our constant turning to God. This is doubly true in a cultural environment that is not likely to recognize and support our true identity in God, indeed, where we can expect the reverse (though God seems to find support for us in very unlikely places).

If you would like to undertake related reading about our spiritual identity, I will mention a few selected works here in a note.[6] More than further reading though, I would encourage you to attend your own firsthand awareness of these different dimensions of self on the journey to your full being in God. Some of the prayer practices in this book I hope will assist you in this attentiveness.

Part 1

LIFE'S DOORS INTO GOD: DIMENSIONS OF SPIRITUAL LIVING

"Where can I go from your Spirit?" Nowhere, as the author of Psalm 139 so powerfully spells out for us. As we turn through different dimensions of daily living, we find that we come face to face with the same deep Reality. Each turn reveals but a different window through which we see and are seen, a different door into the same Divine Mystery through which we move and are moved (and so on through the analogies of all our senses). Thus the process of spiritual formation evolves through every avenue of life.

We can divide this "everything" for better understanding in a myriad of different ways. I have chosen a way of practically attending our spiritual lives through eight particular themes. As you move through these, it is important to remember that they deeply interpenetrate one another. They are not isolated categories. They are dimensions of one dynamic, coinherent life in God. Because of this interpenetration, it is not essential to read the chapters or practice the exercises in their written order (although there are occasional references to comments in previous chapters as we go along). If you are not familiar with an understanding and practice of *discernment* (discerning consonance with God's will in decision-making), you may want to read the section on discernment in chapter 7 (page 99) early on. This may be helpful as you face discernment issues in this book.

CHAPTER 1

Grounding

Sooner or later we sense it. The "it" is hard to describe. Something deep inside is moving. Sometimes we may feel it as a certain restlessness, hunger, or emptiness. At other times we might feel it more positively, as a quality of peace, light, love, or calling.

We can respond in different ways. We might mistake the hunger as a need for more sensual, ego, or superego gratification of some kind. Then we turn our energies to various material, relational, work, or educational pursuits that aim at such gratification. In such ways we strive to fill the hole we feel within us. We may find temporary relief in these ways, but the gnawing feeling inside us has a way of returning. When it does, we may try to ignore it as some psychological quirk not worth paying attention to. We can respond differently though. We can choose to drop deeper and listen more carefully. Then we might begin to sense the restlessness as a fever of our undernourished, deepest nature grown out of that mysterious loving Ground we call God.

If our spiritual fever has had a full rather than empty content, with some sense of peace, love, etc., we may have a confused response. At our sanest we feel deeply drawn to the One who gives the experience. However, our confused egos feel disoriented and out of control. As a result we are tempted to draw the experience toward us as a possession, a trophy to grasp, secure, and assimilate into a willed autonomous empire of self. The sad result is a greater separation from the Holy Source of the experience, who has been inviting us to relinquish our confused and willful autonomy for the sake of deeper communion.

We are made for this deepening, creative, loving, liberating communion. But we are also made in such a way that we are free to miss and resist the invitations. Jews call this tendency a *yetzer hara,* "a wayward heart." Christians call it a divided heart.

The webs of our interior and exterior relationships, social structures, and cultural values spin out of this divided situation. When we see these assisting communion with God and God's creation, our heart in God has been at work. When we see them spinning us away from such communion, our wayward heart has been at work. Since both these forces are active, we can call our human world broken: one full of human pieces broken off in consciousness from their shared Ground and driven in contradictory directions. One direction aims at accumulating mental and material things for ourselves in order to grow larger and more separate (St. Paul's way of the flesh, of sin). The other direction seeks our proper "fit" with God and creation in order to realize dynamic communion (the way of the spirit, of sanctification).

This drama is lived out in special hopefulness when we take seriously God's mysterious power eternally at work for us through the Holy Spirit, working to reconcile our hearts and the world's heart. In Jesus Christ we see our brokenness compassionately exposed and our deepest heart in God empowered. But not fully. The battle continues, but now with a beginning sense of orientation and trust in One who is for us.

Thereafter, for the rest of our lives, we are called to deepen this orientation and trust in all dimensions of our being: our minds, senses, imaginations, wills, bodies, and communities. This is the historic process of ongoing conversion, of sanctification, of living into our shared human call to holiness.

All the authentic historic resources for spiritual formation are aimed at assisting this process in these many dimensions of our being. We would not need such resources if the process was easy and clear cut. We all know by hard experience that it is not. We all live daily with the two questions that a Cistercian abbot once told me that people are always bringing to him:

What do I do?

How am I doing?

These are questions of discernment.[1] In the end we must answer them for ourselves, since we are dealing with a mysterious process of unique unfolding that no one can be closer to than we ourselves. God has never created anyone just like you or me, and the process of unfolding our Christ-nature is distinctive with everyone. There is no clear blueprint known ahead of time to follow, no precast mold into which to pour ourselves. Each of us is an adventure of God's Spirit.

However, this adventure unfolds as part of a *collective* journey. The very nature of God is described as corporate: a loving Three-in-Oneness, reflected in our own being. Further, St. Paul describes us as members of a giant Body of Christ in which our differences are seen as complementary, mysteriously working together toward a common end (1 Cor. 12). Modern physical sciences, too, strongly reinforce an awareness of interdependence and coinherence in the movement of life. Thus we can turn to one another in expectation that, even with all our differences, we have much in common. God's Spirit is reverberated among us in our shared conversation, silence, prayer, and action.

Other spirits are reverberated among us too: spirits of confusion, narrowness, oppression, willfulness, and evil. Thus seeking spiritual help from people and literature around us in itself involves discernment. We need to test the resources we turn to for the fruits of God's Spirit (Gal. 5:22).

What kind of resources do we need for helping us discern and turn to God in our daily lives rather than to the delusions of all the lesser spirits that touch us? Look first to your own experience in answering this question. What resources *have* you turned to in recent years, and with what results? Do some of these seem empty and in need of "benign neglect" now? Do others come to mind that seem particularly called for? Do you sense a call to some new resources?

PRAYER

Later we will be looking at many kinds of resources and support for our spiritual lives. All of these are grounded in that special quality of awareness that is called *prayer*. Authentic prayer is opening to God's gracious presence with all that we are, with what Scripture summarizes as our whole heart, soul, and mind (Matt 22:37). Therefore prayer is more a way of *being* than an isolated act of doing.

Prayer is aimed at our deepest problem: our tendency to forget our liberating connectedness with God. When this happens we become lost in a sense of ultimate separateness. From this narrow outside-of-God place rise our worst fears, cravings, restlessness, and personal and social sinfulness. My colleague Gerald May well states our situation when he says, "The mind is a child of the Spirit, but it likes to run away from home."

Prayer also arises from our deepest hope: for the abundance of life that comes when we abide in our deepest home, our widest consciousness. Prayer is our bridge to Home.

Active prayer is present where our wills normally shape our opening to God, with faint or strong promptings from deep within. Intercession, petition, confession, thanksgiving, and praise are forms of active prayer. These are forms of prayer that most of us learn as children and find reinforced in corporate worship and Scripture. Their content and shape rise naturally out of our daily lives and evolving spiritual life.

Quiet, comtemplative prayer[2] happens when we are still and open ourselves to Christ's Spirit working secretly in us, when we heed the psalmist's plea: "Be still and know that I am God" (Ps. 46:10). These are times when we trustingly sink into God's formless hands for cleansing, illumination, and communion. Sometimes spontaneous sounds and words come through us in such prayer, but more often we are in a state of quiet appreciation, simply hollowed out for God. At the gifted depth of this kind of prayer we pass beyond any image of God and beyond any image of self. We are left in a mutual raw presence. Here we realize that God and ourselves quite literally are more than we can imagine. We need not be bound by our images, however helpful they may be along the way. That is the depth of freedom reflected in the Second Commandment: "You shall not make a graven image . . .and bow down to it" (Exod. 20:4).

THE TRUE SELF IN THE HEART

Such contemplative prayer finds us in what Scripture calls our "hearts": our deepest, truest self in God, the self that is deeper than our normal sense of mind and feelings, yet includes these in a transfigured way. Here is the "home" of God in us, where we are most together, "I pray that Christ will *dwell** in your hearts through faith" (Eph. 3:17). It is the core dimension of our being where we most realize our divinely gifted nature, indeed, where we sense ourselves being intimately breathed in and out by God continually. In the placeless place of the spiritual heart we are in touch before thoughts, beyond thoughts. We can bring into that inner sanctuary only our naked trust and longing.

The heart is a dangerous place to our minds, because there we are dependent upon something—Someone—beyond our control and mental grasp. Our constricted ego self is relativized to this larger Being. Our tendency then is to beat a hasty retreat from the heart back to the mind and its defining images, even though we still feel drawn to the open heart. It is no accident then that the Latin root of our word prayer is *precaria,* "precarious."[3] In heart prayer we are vulnerable, and our trust that God is good is vital if we are to abide there.

This classic movement from the mind to the heart is crucial in spiritual development. It is the biblical movement toward purity of heart. As the anonymous author of the *Cloud of Unknowing* says, "By the heart God can be gotten, by the mind never." Perhaps this might be a little more precisely stated, "By the open heart God can directly get to us, by the mind alone only remotely." We cannot force this movement. It happens as God is ready and we are willing. It is a *graced* movement. But we can invite it and prepare ourselves for it. We can, as St. Symeon the New Theologian said long ago, try to find our heart and abide there.[4]

My guess is that all of us have found our spiritual heart, however faintly. Our problem is *abiding* in its obscurity and letting its fire slowly transfigure all dimensions of our being. If the fundamental spiritual discipline is prayer, opening to God, then the fundamental discipline of prayer is turning to our heart and inviting a sustained mutual pres-

---

*Italics are mine in biblical quotations throughout this book.

ence. Sustaining this presence classically is called "guarding the heart." To paraphrase St. Seraphim of Sarov: "One must constantly guard the heart. The heart cannot live unless it is full of that living water which boils in the heat of the divine fire. When this is poured out, the heart grows cold and becomes like an icicle."[5]

DECEPTION AND HUMILITY

Our minds usually are ahead of the heart in this process. We can have wonderful images for holiness stimulated by our reading and hearing about the tradition. These images resonate with vague stirrings of the Spirit in our hearts. But the water remains tepid. It does not come to a boil in the heat of the divine fire and melt our accretions of hardness and fear. So we are left frustrated between our fine images of how it ought to be and how it actually is. Our mind sees way down the pike to heaven. But our spiritual heart is right here with us on this bumpy road, very erratically pumping real life to us.

When we realize this we can be tempted to fake it. We so much want our mind's images to be realized that we act as if they are possible right now through our own efforts. We demand of ourselves a perfection of attitude and behavior for which we are not yet graced. We see the results in every direction. Toward ourselves we become petty tyrants, invoking overstriving and a consequent sense of failure and guilt, or self-deception, at every turn. From our neighbors (family, friends, co-workers, church, social structures), we demand equal perfection and become constant, harsh judges (spoken or silently). With God in prayer we always wear our Sunday best: trying to look good, even in our confession—never admitting our deep-seated resistance, limitation, and hostility, always promising to do better, never really accepting the dark side of our nature before God and its dependence on God's mercy and timing to bring forward fuller conversion.

The alternative to such painful deception is humility. Humility is the deepest kind of honesty. It involves clear-eyed awareness and acceptance of the way we and the world are. Such awareness can be painful, but it is the pain of compassion, not of demanding and deceptive self-righteousness. It is the recognition of the mysterious brokenness of the world that God meets with an open-armed cross rather than with an army. Such redemptive awareness frees us not to flee the brokenness or to create more of it in our flailing out. We are rather free to face what is there and turn it along with ourselves over to God in prayer, ready to act then in whatever way we may be called and empowered.

This is the way of the Paschal Mystery, of Jesus' death and resurrection, in which we are called to be formed daily: the willingness to see and touch the worst, to trust God's presence even there, and to let ourselves be available to God for whatever good might arise. This is very different from imposing a full blueprint of heaven upon ourselves and the world. It is the willingness rather to live caringly in the broken now, surrounded by all our hopeful images of heaven, watching for the Spirit's faint breeze that slowly stirs our hearts and reveals and empowers the next step along the way.

Spiritual perfection is not found in the fulfillment of any rigid blueprint. It is found rather in the surprising moments of meeting between God's active grace and our spontaneous willingness. All of us know such perfect moments. They are moments lived out of the heart, found scattered through the day like manna falling in the desert. They may be very simple and ordinary moments. Perfection is like that.

THE NATURE OF GOD

Who is God for us in all this? I suspect that the nature of God shifts in our awareness many times during the day, and throughout our lifetimes. Sometimes God is a concept planted in our minds that has no current experiential reality. The concept may have intellectual meaning for us, or it may be very empty. At other times what we call God may be identical with our superegos, an internalization of parental conscience and societal rules which we will be rewarded for following and punished for not: God the Judge. At other times God may be our name for a felt transpersonal presence. This presence sometimes seems awesome, or intimate; sometimes it seems an end-in-itself communion: God our Lover. At still other times God may be an opening pressure on our wills, our Guide, or One whose will we would call upon: our Helper, Healer, Redeemer, Sanctifier. And we may also sense God as the subtle Giver coming through the things and events of our history, environment, and personal capacities: our Creator-Sustainer.

In our moments of subtlest awareness we may sense God as so pervasive that all specific content disappears. God becomes the no-thing, the infinite fullness at the open-ended bottom of our identity, out of which we and the world grow second by second, pulsing life into the cosmos of our bodies and universe. We sense God where before we did not: even in the spaces between our thoughts, in the boring nothing between our excitements, in the darkness as well as the light.

Through all these shifting senses of God we need to pray for a steady trust that is not dependent on either our feelings or our concepts. God may be reflected in these, but not fully revealed. Our dedication is meant for God, who is Loving Truth and Spirit manifesting life in endless ways within and beyond our imagination. Our trust of God needs to be free to soar in us unbound by our attachments to particular images and feelings, just as our sense of God needs to be free to soar unbound by the many other attachments in our lives that in fact are securing substitutes for the Real One.

Over a lifetime we are called to relinquish many such attachments. We all know how hard this is. We need a graced trust if we are to relinquish what we so desperately cling to for security, for the sake of our *real* freedom and security in God. As this happens, we are slowly moved from the latent image of God in which we are born toward the actual likeness of God, for which we were made.[6] Everyone hungers for this movement, however much we may try to deflect it toward more manageable hungers. It reflects our fundamental dynamic nature as literal offspring of the Infinite Wellspring, the nature revealed to us at its transfigured height in Christ's radiant face on Mount Tabor (Matt. 17). In this nature rests our ultimate dignity, and our responsibility of reverencing this divine dignity in others and supporting a social fabric that embodies such respect.

CHAPTER 2

Embodiment

"And [Jesus'] face shone like the sun. . . ." (Matt. 17:2): God enfleshed, the human body transfigured. The Incarnation reveals our enspirited bodies, our embodied spirits, in Christ. Paul develops this: "We are the Temple of the Living God" (2 Cor. 6:16). "Glorify God in your body" (1 Cor. 6:20). Attention to the body is integral to spiritual life.

Yet our physical form is an ambiguous embodiment of the Spirit. It is subject to degeneration and brings a mixture of pain and pleasure. Its passions can twist us away from God as well as open us to God. St. Paul realizes this ambiguity in many ways, but he never rejects the body's place in the spiritual life (Rom. 8:4ff.). His contrast of "the way of the flesh" and "the way of the spirit" has suffered much distortion historically. Contemporary biblical scholarship makes it clear that Paul does not contrast physical body and spirit, but rather contrasts ways of life that are oriented away or toward God.[1]

We all know how easily our bodily passions can stimulate our willful little ego self into its self-absorbed tyranny, often resulting in one of the seven deadly sins.[2] But the same energy that stokes such passions can become compassion, i.e., "willing for God" passions. Thus it is not a matter of suppressing one kind of bodily energy and replacing it with another. It is rather a question of which way this one raw, vibrant energy within us is turned. The turn toward compassion is a turn toward God, with God's help and our willingness.

The ground for all spiritual disciplines of the body is our intent to keep ourselves available for God. This will entail guidance toward openness rather tightness, balance rather than grabbiness, alertness rather than scatteredness. This process involves our body, mind, and spirit as different foci of one linked reality. St. Anthony long ago spoke to this linkage:

This Spirit, combining with the mind . . . teaches it to keep the body in order—all of it, from head to foot: the eyes to see with purity; the ears, to listen in peace, not to delight in slander, gossip and abuse; the tongue, to say only what is good; . . . the hands, to be raised in prayer and for works of mercy . . .; the stomach, to keep the use of food and drink within the necessary limits . . . ; the feet, to walk rightly and follow the will of God. . . . In this way the whole body becomes trained in good and undergoes a change, submitting to the rule of the Holy Spirit, so that in the end it begins in some measure to share in such properties of the spiritual body, as it is to receive at the resurrection of the just.[3]

The body is a gift and vehicle of God, integral to our being. Seeing its physical and spiritual dimensions united draws us into a sense of the Body of Christ, that cosmic divine embodiment (Eph. 1:23) we share together. I do not use this term metaphorically, but literally. I believe we share in integral physical-spiritual reality with God, revealed to us in Christ. The wonder of this deepens further when we sense that in some way our embodied nature itself is like a hologram of that cosmic Body: within us is a universe of interwoven space, form, and spirit, grown and pervaded by God's Spirit in Christ. As we move to more concrete dimensions of the body now, we need to remember this larger perspective that shows us what a precious, awesome, divine expression we are in our embodiment.[4]

BODY PRAYER

Anything we do with our bodies is a form of prayer when our central intent is opening to God's presence through it. Much attention is paid to the body in contemporary Western culture, but the intent rarely is prayer. Even in the church we have tended to categorize the body as something outside the orbit of intentional spiritual formation. Prayer for healing, for example, tends to focus on getting the body well again as an end in itself, rather than as a means of deepening life in God. Jesus lamented such an attitude when only one leper returned to give praise to God (Luke 17:18). Dieting is usually undertaken exclusively for reasons of physical health rather than within the context of fasting to become more available to God. The body, both in and out of the church, tends to be approached in terms of physical fitness and beauty apart from a direct relationship to God.

On the other hand the body may simply be ignored as a positive force. We can be very hard on our bodies, as when we get high on alcohol or drugs, work too hard, or ignore the body's need for sleep and exercise. The body is treated violently and contemptuously in such cases for the sake of some goal of pleasure or achievement.

This tendency is matched by an older and now often unpopular Christian asceticism of the body which would deny bodily needs for the sake of giving fuller service to others, or in order to come closer to an awareness of God. In extreme form such ascetical practices can interfere both with alert service and with God-awareness, yet this tradition contains within it seeds of truth going back to Jesus' passion, and to certain declarations of St. Paul (e.g., 1 Cor. 9:27 JB: "I treat my body hard and make it obey me [so I won't be disqualified from the race]," and Rom. 6:19: "put your bodies at the service of righteousness for your sanctification").

Certain Eastern religious traditions over the years have stimulated my understanding of the possibilities for body prayer, to the extent that they have attended the body's spiritual dimensions much more carefully than we usually have in the West. One of the ironies of history, one of God's endless surprises, is the way many Christians today find themselves turning to hatha yoga and other practices precisely because they find help for more fully living out an incarnational Christian faith that values the human body as a divine gift and vehicle.

The lack of adequate equivalent resources in the West is due to a variety of influences, including early cultural and philosophical ones that led to a separation of body and soul, a relative demeaning of the body, and misinterpretation of St. Paul's "way of the flesh" as meaning the way of the body. There were many exceptions to this, as mentioned earlier, and the influential Rule of St. Benedict gave a strong practical place to physical labor in the way to God.[5] Yet it would seem that only in recent decades has the church more generally and fully begun to recover a Hebraic view of the body's integral place in our spiritual nature.

Whatever the many historical reasons, the West has been relatively impoverished in approaching the body comprehensively and carefully as a means of attending God. Western body awareness has gone in different directions: either toward supersophistication in understanding the body as a material mechanism, or as an instrument of pleasure, in both cases usually outside any intentional spiritual purpose.

In the wider ecumenism of the Spirit being opened for us today, we need to humbly accept the learnings of particular Eastern religions in relation to the body now available to us. What makes a particular practice Christian is not its source, but its *intent*. If our intent in assuming a particular bodily practice is to deepen our awareness in Christ, then it is Christian. If this is not our intent, then even the reading of Scripture loses its authenticity.

I say this in the context of the long history of Christian spiritual practice which has included utilization of methods and vocabulary that have originated out of many nonspecifically Christian sources. The Bible itself is full of such influences. This is important to remember in the face of those Christians who would try to impoverish our spiritual resources by too narrowly defining them. If we view the human family as one in God's Spirit, then this historical cross-fertilization is not surprising, nor is it the same as a patched-together eclecticism. We realize that God's mysterious Spirit is profligate in the world, creating God-consciousness in endless forms. A faith and understanding of God in

Christ gives Christians a distinctive interior center from which to discern and embrace this divine Presence wherever it is genuinely manifest. In terms of the body, selective attention to Eastern spiritual practices can be of great assistance to a fully embodied Christian life. They also can provide challenge to the secularization of the body dominant in Western science and common life.

I have divided the body's ways of assisting our presence to God into six areas: posture, breath, movement, gesture, clothing, and diet. Discussion of other dimensions of the body will be found scattered throughout other chapters. In reading through these and other practices in this book, it is necessary to remember that none of our efforts are *essential* to God's graced presence. That presence exists apart from our efforts. However, these methods can help us to do what we can from the human side (that is the meaning of ascetical practice). They can help us to notice rather than miss the grace at hand, and to allow the grace to be integrated into our ongoing way of life.

POSTURE

How do we position our bodies in prayer? The basic answer is any way that allows us to be relaxed and energetically attentive. If we are going to be in prayer for a long time, then I would add: in whatever position we can maintain, without the body contributing to distraction through discomfort or drowsiness. Once we are in such a position, we find that our bodies are inviting our minds to be likewise: relaxed, attentive, willing to be present a long time, permeable to the Spirit.

STATIONARY POSITIONS

There is no one right position for this, even for the same person all of the time. We might experiment with sitting, kneeling, lying down, and standing. All these have their potential place at one time or another. However, for *sustained* prayer, for most people most of the time, a sitting posture will likely be best. If we are going to sustain this position without distraction, we need to sit up straight, with backs and necks in line but not tense. If we choose a chair rather than the floor, our feet should be flat on the floor. A straight-backed chair will likely be best, though even many of these can give us difficulty because of their height or slope. We need to search for one in which our body can really feel alertly at ease.

If we choose to sit on the floor, the best assistance I know of is a prayer bench, with a beveled top that helps the back and neck to be straight and in line. Our legs are in a kneeling position, tucked under the bench. These benches can be handmade or purchased.[6] The reasons they are growing in popular use today include the relative ease with which the legs and back can be dealt with, the symbolically prayerful posture that it allows, and the sense of humble yet confident grounding that sitting on the floor embodies.

The alternative way of sitting on the floor involves the use of a firm, thick cushion or its equivalent, sitting toward the forward edge where the back and neck spontaneously fall in line. The legs ideally are folded, with one heel between the legs, and the knees touching the floor for stability. This is fine for people with limber legs. For others eventual pain or numbness in the legs can become a distraction.

Whatever the position, it is helpful to keep the body still. Each movement can become a distraction, a way of pulling out of our deepening presence. However, a certain flexibility is called for with this rule: too rigid an approach, where we sit in fearful determination not to move, can also become distracting. The important point is not to make too big a deal out of moving or not moving, but where we sense a choice, remaining still. A still body invites a still, receptive mind.

STRETCHING POSITIONS

Besides sitting postures there are those particular stretching positions that are called *asanas* in hatha yoga. These are often taught in the West simply as a secular form of relaxation and physical fitness. However, if our intent is opening to God through them, they can have a powerful capacity to help us drop beneath the surface scatteredness and tension to a prayerful presence. Behind hatha yoga lies thousands of years of experience with bringing the body to such presence. Throughout East Asian traditions there runs an assumption that in and around us is a subtle energy, called *prana* in Sanskrit, *chi* in Chinese, *ki* in Japanese. Opening the channels of this energy enables a beginning state of calm spiritual attentiveness. This energy has many healing and spiritual purposes in Eastern traditions that are outside our simple concern here for bodily wakefulness.

There are hatha yoga positions for influencing every inch of our bodies, inside and out, with hundreds of variations. For the purposes of assisting our prayer we need only a few of these. If they are being used in groups as described in the last chapter, they should be simple. Complicated ones tempt competition and can become distracting. I mention a few positions and some reading resources in my book, *Living Simply Through the Day*.[7] Others out of Tibetan tradition can be found in *Kum Nye Relaxation*.[8]

In groups, two or three different positions might be introduced in a given session and repeated for one or two more sessions. Introduction of too many at one time, or too many during the life of a group, also can prove distracting, drawing too much attention to the body per se rather than drawing us to a simple, open prayerful presence. Instructions need to be clear and succinct, surrounded by silence.

Over the length of a group's life participants might find a few positions that are particularly opening for them. These can be continued on a daily basis. They often prove excellent ways into daily prayer time. Our minds often are resistant to taking that time, perhaps due to a compulsion to keep busy and a fear of losing control. Beginning with one or more stretching positions has a way of loosening the mind's drivenness and freeing us to really remain there and become more directly present to God, as we are spiritually ready. Attention to the breath to which we now will turn can also serve this purpose.

BREATH

Breathing is fundamental to our physical being. In Scripture it is a symbol of life from Genesis (God breathed life into Adam: Gen. 2:7) through Revelation ("a breath of life from God entered them": Rev. 11:11). More specifically it becomes a symbol of God's life, God's Spirit, God's holy Wind (*ruach* in Hebrew, *pneuma* in Greek) inspiring life.

Physical breath is a very apt symbol of God's Spirit and our spirit. Breath is invisible to the naked eye, yet it is very real and powerful. It cleanses, enlivens, and calms us. It cannot be confined in one place. It has a dynamic quality of movement, drawing on the air that pervades us inside and out. Breath reveals the illusion in any sense of ultimate self-isolation and separateness: we are always drawing it into us and returning it, demonstrating the fluidity of our embodiment, its literal interdependence with the rest of life. Breath is *our* breath, and yet it is not: it is air that we cannot possess. Such physical realities help us to understand the subtle intimacy of our human-divine interconnectedness.

More practically, attention to our breathing provides the simplest physical means of releasing a crowded, tense surface of mind and body. The most fundamental point is to slow down the breath. The more shallow and high in the chest we breathe, the more rapidly we breathe. Such rapid shallow breathing usually both reflects and reinforces tension in us. This in turn has a way of stimulating rapid, shallow thoughts that match the breathing. Our minds are racing. One thought feeds another in a driven, panicky way. There is no room for the deeper Spirit to get through to us. We are tied up in producing an ever taller mental junk heap that takes the place of God.

Even when we want to relinquish this pattern, we sometimes find that the physical process is so strong and reinforcing that we cannot. We might instinctively draw in a deep breath and sigh, our body's way of pointing the way out for us. We can take this hint and go farther. Exercise 1 is one way of opening to God through slowing the breath.

EXERCISE 1: BREATHING OPEN

1. Lightly notice the speediness of your breath and thoughts.
2. Remember your desire for God in the form of a prayer or wordless feeling.
3. Begin breathing slowly deep down into your diaphragm-stomach area. You can put your hands on this area and feel it swell out with your in-breath. Gradually fill your lungs from this bottom point upward.
4. Hold the breath briefly, but without closing your throat.
5. Release your breath very slowly, twice as slowly as you breathed in. Pause at the bottom of your breath briefly with a very still mind.
6. Continue this rhythm of breathing for a few minutes or longer, but now with the specific intent of breathing in all that is of God, and breathing out all in your body and mind that is not. You need not think of anything in terms of content; just retain a naked *intent* to be filled from head to toe with all that is of God, and to release whatever may come between you and God. In the process let your body and mind sink beneath the crowded, surface tension to that more spacious and free place where you are confidently grounded in God.

Steps 3 through 5 can be eliminated as separate from step 6 after you have become familiar with this basic way of breathing. With less exaggeration than described here, this kind of breathing can become your *normal* way of breathing most of the time, even with many forms of physical exercise (at least this is true in my own experience). Such breathing then can become a regular means of heading off or releasing those grabby tensions and speediness of mind and body that easily take our awareness away from God. Breathing becomes a fundamental spiritual exercise that is available all the time.

Perhaps St. Paul would understand this and other forms of bodily discipline in light of his pleas to "make every part of your body into a weapon fighting on the side of God" (Rom. 6:13, JB). However, we are speaking of very gentle weapons here that do not directly attack physical-mental antagonists, but rather transform their dividing power into calmed, available energy for God.

REFLECTION QUESTIONS

Alone or in small groups, you can reflect on such questions as these:

1. Did the slow breathing seem to make any difference to your presence for God?
2. Can you think of ways that your breathing habits and mental associations with breath have drawn you toward or away from presence for God?
3. What implications might this exercise have for your daily living?

MOVEMENT

We can have this same intent in our physical movement. St. Paul's words can be taken literally when he says, "If we live by the Spirit, let us also *walk* by the Spirit" (Gal. 5:25)! Walking and other forms of movement have a way of being "secularized": they are things we do between ways of attending God and life in God. They are a kind of "time out" between the "real" things, a way of unconsciously passing from one thing to another. In highly rushed societies and communities, this attitude is particularly prevalent. Our minds decide where we want to go. Anything along the way is but a means to or an interference with this command. We are in control and aim to stay that way.

Such societal habits easily miss the grace along the way. Emily Dickinson put it best: "Instead of getting to heaven at last / I am going all along."[9] The Reign of God is being realized on earth as in heaven— step by step. We move on pilgrimage, which is both moving with God and toward God, trusting God on a path that is mysterious and unknown in advance. The mystery of the path means that we need to stay alert, for the Holy One may appear at any time, and at any place. There is not any "no-God's land" along the way. It is all God's land, every step of the way.

Thus our physical movement itself becomes a spiritual discipline, a time of moving with grace. We have heard that "moving gracefully" is to be desired in a secular, aesthetic sense: a way of moving slowly, easefully, with dignity. Buried behind this term somewhere in the remote past perhaps lies the deeper intent of moving with grace, i.e., moving with the grace at hand: not striding ahead of it in willfulness, or meandering behind it in dullness or narrow self-preoccupation.

In this sense we might speak of an orthodox walk! Striding willfully ahead would reflect that works-righteous heresy that tries to will its way to heaven. Meandering listlessly behind perhaps indicates a heresy that doesn't believe in God's active, calling presence in the moment. It is amazing what a simple walk can reveal!

I know that I fall into both heresies again and again every day, and my walk exposes me.

How can our movement help us to pay attention to the grace at hand? Just as with breathing, the slowness of movement is fundamental. This doesn't mean that grace cannot be noticed when we move fast, anymore than it cannot be noticed when we breathe rapidly! But in moving slowly we are more likely not to miss, and hopefully will enhance, our sensing of God's presence.

Think of the way we walk when we are on retreat. Almost certainly we find ourselves slowing down. Nothing seems quite so incongruous as a group of people fast-hoofing it around a retreat center! Why is this so? I think because we know we are on retreat to pay more careful attention to God's presence, and instinctively we reduce the self-generated speed of our bodies and minds so we can notice that subtle reality more readily. We know there is no self-designed place to drive ourselves toward on an authentic retreat. We are there precisely to release that "in charge" manner and listen for the real Presence here now, moment by moment, inviting us to drop through surface time to its deep dimension in God. So we move slowly, opening time to its easily hidden Heart. We see the same slowness in liturgical processions as well, ultimately for the same reason.

More precisely, we need to move evenly, gracefully, aware that every movement of leg, arm, and head is centered in God, not outside. This may seem self-conscious at first, but its intent is just the opposite: to join our consciousness with the Consciousness that draws us forward, blending our movement in this larger Movement. In this way we realize the true dignity, the divine dignity, of our movement. Any other intent of movement shrinks us to a much smaller, isolated, and finally tragic reality, outside the One in whom we are called to "live and *move* and have our being" (Acts 17:28).

We can bring such graced movement to all kinds of activities besides retreats, if not always as unambiguously as there. It can be encouraged in many little ways: giving ourselves a few extra minutes to drive, ride, or walk somewhere; turning and moving our bodies smoothly instead of jerkily in response to telephones, appointments, physical labor, etc. (a jerked around body encourages a jerky, fragmented mind); playing a sport or using an artistic medium in a way that our movement retains a certain unforced ease, as in jogging and painting. In the process of such movement we will likely be more capable of noticing and carrying out what is really called for at a given time, for our neighbor and ourselves.

I would recommend several martial arts as especially helpful in the cultivation of such graced movement, including t'ai chi and aikido. The latter has the added benefit of offering a way of self-defense that, at least in its founder's intent, remains compassionate toward the aggressor, thus carrying out the spirit of Jesus' injunction to turn the other cheek (Matt. 5:39). This is not irrelevant to graced movement, which has a way of flowing with what is present in an involved, discerning way. Ungraced movement, on the other hand, has a divisive, polarizing quality to it. We move out of touch with the grace at hand, which leaves us with a reality confined to our little ego's fears and drives. We are far more likely then to become an aggressor, or to flee when we are called to stand firm.

Finally, let me offer a particular intensive exercise (exercise 2: Going Without Leaving Home) that can be used by a group or an individual to help condition this capacity for moving more in touch with the grace at hand.[10]

EXERCISE 2: GOING WITHOUT LEAVING HOME

1. If in a group, stand in a circle, at least an arm's length apart. If you are alone, make sure you have enough space to walk in a circle or straight path without encumbrance.
2. Take several long, slow breaths while praying for an intimate awareness of God's presence.
3. Turn to your left, so that you will be moving clockwise.
4. Extremely slowly and evenly, lift your left foot about six inches off the ground with a sense of lightness. Bring it forward just half a step, so that after your toes touch the ground, your left heel comes down at the instep of your right foot. Now lift your right foot in the same slow, even manner. Keep your eyes unfocused, on the ground several feet ahead of you.
5. Let your mind, breath, and movement continually flow together as one. If your mind falls behind in memory, ahead in anticipation, or outside as an observer, gently let it rejoin the slow, present flow of breath and movement again. Sense the spacious inclusiveness of the present moment.
6. At times, as you breathe in you can slowly lift your arms to a horizontal position; hold this position for a step or two (but don't hold your breath), then let them descend on an out-breath.
7. Continue this very slow movement for at least twenty minutes; twice that long if you can. If you easily lose your balance, see if you can keep your mind steady even then. If you lift your foot less your balance will become easier. It can also be helped by sensing the movement as guided effortlessly from the center of your body rather than effortfully from your head.
8. Return to your original place now at a somewhat faster pace, and

sit in silence for at least five minutes with the same open-to-God mind.

REFLECTION QUESTIONS

1. Did you notice the difference between moments when (a) every-thing was un–self-consciously together, a sense of moving will-ingly and directly in the flow of the Spirit? (b) your mind fell behind, ahead, or outside, creating a sense of lostness, willful ef-fort, judgment, distance, or awkwardness? Were you able to re-main given to God in those times?
2. When you think of the way you normally move through the day, can you sense a desire to move in a way that is more of an aid and less of a hindrance to your flow with the grace at hand? Can you pray for this to be empowered?

You may feel a restless impatience at times during this exercise if it is done as described. This may be the slowest you have ever moved for such a long period. You might note how much our minds desire dis-traction, striving for goals, and entertainment. Yet movement needs to be boring if you are to be brought fully into the moment with God, boring in the sense of inviting recollection rather than agitated grasping for something more. Such presence can lead to a sense of sufficiency and richness, of being at home in God as you move, rather than a sense of impoverishment that drives you out of the given moment, God's moment.

When we are fully present in the flow of the moment, time and eternity have a way of collapsing into one another: eternity is sensed as the depth, the fullness of time. The whole creation rises together, joined in God; there are only dotted lines, if any at all, between past, present, and future.

Joggers, swimmers, and dancers sometimes seem to have a beginning taste of this eternity in the moment when they suddenly sense they are moving and yet not moving at the same time, but they rarely have a spiritual context that allows them to carry the experience into its full depth and implications.

The spiritual context for movement, among other things, can draw out of us a certain healthy repentance. We come to see how much we need to loosen the overly controlling, distracted nature of our minds and prefer more simple attention to God's unfolding presence, which is the source of our true self, freedom, vocation, and joy. Such liber-ating repentance begins with prayer for its empowerment.

GESTURE

"Then [Jesus] went down on his knees and prayed. . . ."(Luke 23:41). Going down on our knees is one way our bodies participate in prayer. It is an example of a spiritually meaningful position, a gesture, that invites our mind and heart to a prayerful presence, or reinforces their already existent prayerfulness.

Godfrey Diekman, a Benedictine liturgical scholar, once wrote of the three primary gestures of the Eucharist: standing to express our dignity and shared mission in Jesus Christ, kneeling to express the transcendence of God our Creator/Father/Mother, and touching to express the Holy Spirit's life conveyed through us.[11] We find such touching in the exchange of Peace, and outside the Eucharist in laying on hands for healing, reconciliation, ordination, commissioning, and in baptism. Outside of a liturgical context such a sacramental touching can be present, when that is our intent, in hugs, handshakes, or smiles of real caring for anyone.

Historically, we find a host of other spiritual gestures, including bowing, genuflection, prostration, lighting a candle, holding our hands in particular ways, and making a sign of the cross. Eastern Orthodox tradition adds the kissing of icons, touching the earth (as a sign of humility), and even moving up the steps into church as a gesture of moving toward heaven. At a certain point in the history of the Hesychastic Jesus Prayer tradition, the gesture of bowing one's head and looking at the center of the body during prayer was encouraged.[12]

The long, rich history of gesture in Christian tradition is reinforced and expanded when we look at its wide practice in other deep religious traditions. Meaningful gesture can unite mind and body and present us whole to God. It is deeply embedded in the human psyche as a means of prayerful presence.

One gesture that many people find helpful during long prayer times relates to our hands. It is amazing what a difference the position of our hands can make to prayer. If we pray with arms folded, it has a way of tempting our minds to fold away from participation. If we pray with our hands tightly interlocked, this invites a tensely present mind. If we pray with our arms raised, the classic Hebraic gesture, our minds, too, are invited to be raised to God, but when we are praying for a long time the strain of keeping the arms up can become a distraction.

What I have found most helpful for people is to sit with their hands loosely open, resting on top of their knees, or open on top of each other in their laps. This gesture can be held for a long time, and its open quality invites the mind to be likewise before God.

Beyond this, as we move through the day and week we might want to pay a little closer attention to the impact of bodily gesture on our prayerful presence. We may already have semi-conscious gestures that either impede or enhance our prayer, or we may need to cultivate a few more positive ones.

CLOTHING

Normally we think of clothing only as what we wear next to our bodies. But we are clothed in another way: by a particular material environment, indoors or outside. What kind of environment most invites our prayerful presence? For most of us most of the time this will likely entail a place that is quiet, simple, familiar, and with some inviting focus for our eyes such as a light-colored candle, cross, icon, Bible, bowl of water, stone, or flower. The quietness helps us settle down; the simplicity eases distraction; the familiarity reduces anxiety; the focus gives us a way of drawing our attention to God. Other aspects of the environment also can affect our prayer: temperature, time of day, hills, valleys, water, wind. Each of us can note what difference these might make for our quality of presence.

In terms of the clothes we wear, we can ask ourselves if it makes any difference to our prayerful presence whether or not our clothing is simple or complicated, cheap or expensive, loose or tight, ordinary or special (as when we wear a uniform). We might also note what difference it makes to wear particular art objects: crosses, jewelry, etc. I know people who occasionally change the arms on which they wear their watch or ring, or carry a small stone or other object in their pocket, as physical reminders of God's presence.

We might also notice what difference it makes to pray with or without shoes. Christian tradition is one of the very few deep religious traditions in which shoes usually are kept on during prayer. Personally I find a little more humility brought on by bare feet; I feel like there is one less thing standing between me and God. This is pressed all the way when we find ourselves praying completely naked, as in the shower. When nothing is hidden physically, perhaps we feel more free to hide nothing in our mental prayer. We come to God just as we are. We might also find greater self-acceptance of our bodies before God.

These environmental influences are not always that significant to our prayerful presence, but it is amazing how at times they can add up in a way that genuinely opens or blocks such presence. Our minds often are delicately balanced between wanting to be deeply present to God and wanting to be just perfunctorily present, or not present at all. Thus we need to pay attention to whatever might help tilt the balance in God's favor.

DIET

The summary of the Law (Matt. 22:36ff.), so fundamental a declaration about the way to life in Judeo-Christian tradition, tells us to love

God with our whole being, and our neighbor as ourself. When we come to food, all three dimensions are present: personal health, morality, and direct presence to God. As we examine each of these, we need to remember the universal witness of the world's deep religions to the significance of food in the process of the spiritual life, and its voluntary withdrawal in fasting.

The dimension of diet that serves our direct turning to God is the proper subject of this book. However, the health and moral aspects are so often confused or interwoven with it that I want to dwell on those first so that I can more easily draw out the distinctively spiritual quality of fasting. This isn't to say that these other dimensions are any less important, but simply that we cannot collapse the explicitly spiritual dimension into them without loss of an important historical intent. That intent, as with all spiritual disciplines, is direct attention to God.

PHYSICAL HEALTH

"A monk should live as if he were to die tomorrow, but at the same time treat the body as if he were to live on with it for many years to come."

This statement by Palladius in the early Church contains wisdom for us all. It helps us distinguish bodily care from narcissistic overconcern. The body indeed is a precious gift and what we put into it should witness to this. Our minds are stewards of our bodies. Disregarding our stewardship violates respect for this gift. At the same time, we need to avoid the modern fetish of the body, wherein we become so identified with it, and so afraid of becoming ill, flabby, or dead, that we in effect create an idol that comes between us and God. Then we mistake the body for all that we are; we forget that we are embodied spirits, growing out of Spirit.

Our physical bodies are penultimate to their enspirited nature, however integral they are in some form to this nature. Just as painted icons are more than paint and wood, so our nature is more than flesh and blood. We are icons of God. Thus we can be prepared to die to our earthly physical frame tomorrow, trusting to God for the mysterious embodied life that is promised thereafter.

We are free to spend our bodies for God's joy and peace in the world, however this might be called for, paying attention to what will keep them fit along the way the best way we can. This means a certain moderation, and where there is a choice, selecting those foods that we really think our body needs. It means not doing unnecessary violence to our bodies in what we eat and drink, or doing anything that diverts our central attention from God.

Fasting (eating no food) and abstinence (withdrawal from certain kinds of food) have physical as well as moral and spiritual implications. One of the most sensible kinds of fast in my experience, for whatever reason it is undertaken, is a juice fast for a few days. This involves a glass of fruit or vegetable juice three times a day, and nothing more except water. Liquids are important during a fast to keep us from dehydration. Some people feel it is good to ease into and out of such a fast by cutting down your meals a day or two ahead of time, and gradually resuming your normal diet over a day or two after the fast.[13]

MORAL CONCERN

Eating or fasting with moral concern is to eat or fast with our neighbor in mind. Our neighbor is involved in our diet in the following three ways.

1. *Ecology*. There is a wonderful bumper sticker that has a picture of the earth with the caption, "Love your mother!" This planet in a sense is part of our larger body. And so are the generations of people who will follow us. We need to grow and consume food in ways that will insure replenishing of the earth's ecosystem.

2. *Sharing of Resources*. We also need to support ways of growing and distributing food resources so that enough is available for everyone on this planet. Most of us are familiar with this dimension of food; it is a classic and visible concern of the Church rooted in many passages of Scripture, culminating in Jesus' mystical identification of himself with the hungry ("I was hungry and you gave me food . . ." Matt. 25:35). Fasting has a way of reminding us of the hungry and helping us to identify with them.

3. *Expressing Community*. Corporate feasting and fasting times were established very early in the Church liturgical year in recognition of great people and events of salvation history. Since food is such a very basic part of human experience, such days bring this activity into the conscious collective orbit of grace: either grace to be celebrated at feasts or to be sought in fasts. One advantage of such a corporate fast over a private one is that we are less tempted by spiritual pride: everyone else is doing it, too, so we're not so special. (Of course, we can still end up with *group* pride in relation to other groups who don't fast!)

Besides this more formal communal dimension, diet becomes an arena for moral community in other ways. It can be utilized for political impact, aimed at the moral conscience of the people. We see this in the famous fasts of people like Mohandas Gandhi, Martin Luther King, Jr., Dick Gregory, and Cesar Chavez. There is a whole network of people who fast for nuclear disarmament. In one of the earliest writings of the Church, the Didache, we are told to "fast for your persecutors." Such fasting reinforces a nonviolent context for needed political change, and it can help to morally purify the one who fasts. If others know you are fasting, it may help in their purification as well.

However, there are risks in others knowing. The one who fasts is in greater danger of turning from God to self importance and manipulation. The persecutors may become more oppressive rather than less. Careful discernment is needed before publicizing a fast. In this same vein of moral community we can add the popular tradition of fasting during Lent and other times for the sake of particular causes, including the giving of money saved to those causes.

Another communal dimension of food has to do with its preparation. We can cook not just as a mechanical chore, but in a mindful way of caring for others who will be fed by this food. We also can occasionally bring in a special religious dimension through giving foods symbolic shapes and colors related to liturgical seasons and meanings. Lenten hot cross buns and Easter breads and eggs are classic examples.[14] The preparation of food further can remind us of our co-creativity with God and one another: God gives the raw materials through the processes of nature, and a succession of collaborative human hands and ingenuity bring these to us in particular forms. We in turn provide a final shaping of these foods for the table.

Finally, diet can become a sign of promise. When we have a meatless fast, it can be undertaken as an eschatological sign of hope for the full community, the peaceable divine Commonwealth where wolf and lamb will lie down together with no more killing, the messianic banquet that has a place for all.

DIRECTLY TURNING TO GOD

When we fast, the relinquishment of our normal grasping for physical fullness can free space for attention to God. We become free to sink more clearly and steadily to our deepest hunger for God. Then hunger for food can later become a desire that is caught up in God, connected with our deepest hunger.

Food then becomes an opportunity for *remembering* God's presence, for giving thanks, and for sharing food as heavenly mana, recalling how often meals with Jesus were occasions of revelation and calls to sharing. Bread itself is a symbol of the Messiah in Scripture, the one who is given us as the Bread of Heaven. The Eucharist is rooted in this Living Bread. Grace at meals is a remembrance of this pervasive divine presence for us.

More concretely, fasting provides a time of freedom from the potential constraints and diversions of having to prepare meals and eat them. It draws us toward simplicity. Further, in my experience the relinquishment of immediate impulses to eat can have a way of reducing the grasping in my mind for all kinds of things. A fallout of this relinquishment I have found is a less violent mind, one content to just be calmly present without restlessly trying to consume more. A certain sufficiency and ease of the moment emerges. There is room for God to rise lightly in consciousness and for the heaviness of ego to subside. Perhaps Evagrius, in the early Church, had such an impact in mind when he advocated "refusing with joy bodily pleasure for the sake of a calm soul of love."

Such spiritual fasting is not something to arbitrarily take on just because we want to or think we should try it out. Our motivation needs to be more than that. It needs to be a response to the call and love of God, and a desire to be led more deeply into that Presence. Perhaps the call involves something more specific, such as the need to prepare the way for the Spirit's healing, or for vocational vision. In any case, it is a potential discipline we need to take to prayer in order to discern its appropriateness for us at a given time. In prayer you can ask to be shown where the drive to fast is coming from. When you think of fasting do you have a sense of openness, love, and being freely drawn? Or does it seem to come more from a little ego source such as curiosity, desire to achieve, or pleasing of others?

Fasting is illustrative of the whole arena of relinquishment in the spiritual life. Robert Pelton says it well: "the deepest fast is from sin. It is above all the mind and heart that need to be cleansed by surrendering the illusory foods they love to feed on."[15] I would add to this our need to fast from the numerous distractions of contemporary life with which we are bombarded, the sensory overload that leaves us numb and stuffed with incoherent bits and pieces. Someone recently suggested fasting from electricity (and batteries) for a while (and therefore all that runs on them) as a particularly appropriate contemporary fast. That could reduce sensory input enormously and leave us more free to be present to a few savored things, drawn to their depth in God.

Fasting overflows into those two other basic disciplines advocated in the Gospels: charity and prayer. These, like fasting, symbolize large arenas of practice. Together these shape our availability to God, our neighbor and our deeper identity in God.

EXERCISE 3: FASTING AND FEASTING

This is a short exercise for groups or individuals, related to diet.

1. Close your eyes and let foods pass through your imagination; sense God's blessing coming to you through them.
2. Now desire God both through and beyond this food, ending in an open, quiet mutual presence where you are "feeding" on God alone.

REFLECTION

Reflect on your own experience, anxiety, and desire related to fasting, normal eating, and feasting as spiritual disciplines. How has food become a way to, and substitute for, God in your life?

If you are feeling the possible edge of a particular new calling in this area, you can go through the steps of discernment suggested in exercise 22.

CHAPTER 3

Sound and Silence

In the beginning was the Word, the Sound, the Vibration of God. Scripture points to the many ways this Sound continues to shape and guide life. There are special sounds for everything in religious history. Many of these focus on symbolic meanings, such as the words of Scripture, liturgy, theology, and the names of God. These are the sounds that normally come to mind when we think of God-related sounds. But there is another dimension of sound in religious history, one that focuses directly on the vibration before any symbolic meaning might emerge.

This dimension is experienced when we hear bells, drums, or other musical instruments. Beethoven once said, in effect, that music is a fuller way to God than words. We also experience the communicative power of vibration itself in nature: the sound of birds, waterfalls, and the wind. Remember that sound of a gentle breeze through which Elijah experienced God, and the earthquake and the cataracts that were vehicles for the psalmists. Then there is the long history of chant, East and West, wherein the impact of the particular tones themselves are meant to affect us.

Such intrinsic sound qualities have a way of opening us deeper into God's mystery, before which all our words fall short. They can draw us beyond our mind's cognitive relation with God to the involvement of our whole being in a more direct, pristine presence in God.

A Benedictine community has made into a chant the great question in the Upanishads 1:1: "Who is it that hears behind the ear . . . ?" When we sink back into the Reality behind this question, we can become present in open wonder and trust of the One who hears and sounds through us, the One who is the ultimate heart of sound. The busy grasping of our minds for sounds as discrete objects and meanings subsides for the moment. God's sounding can more easily come through then in a way that is cleansing, opening, illumining.

Our very lives could be portrayed as vibrations, distinct sounds of God. As modern science has shown us, sound waves shape visible forms, images. God's sound, God's Word shapes us into a particular image of God. We are like particular risings out of the pulsing heart of God. We become stringed instruments of God through which the Holy One continues to vibrate. We are drawn toward dynamic harmony with the larger creation as part of God's universal symphony of sound.

Yet that is not the full picture. There is disharmony, sometimes willful, sometimes ignorant, permitted in God's design. There are regular "harmonic" sounds, but there also are dissonant ones that may be the result of our ego dissonance, or even of some demonic force disrupting us. The demonic represents those forces most willfully cut off from their ultimate source and design in God. Thus sound includes an ambiguous quality. It can be a sign of division between us, God, and God's creation, or it can reflect and empower our unity.

Finally there is the great mystery of silence in relation to sound. Silence can be very attractive to us. Something about it draws us deeper into reality: its stillness, its openness, its gentleness. As we feel its pull on us, though, we also find that we are afraid of silence. We fear its lack of boundaries and its seeming emptiness. We don't know if we can trust what will happen if we let go into it; we wonder if there will be anything left of us if we fully join the silence.

Thus we have a tendency to become very noisy inside to compensate for the silence outside. We want to create shapes in face of the shapelessness of silence. We trust form, we identify with form. Formlessness is much harder to accept as real and full. Very little in our human culture or popular religious life today prepares us to believe otherwise. As a result we often stop ourselves short when we are being lured into the spacious silence.

But there is much in contemplative tradition to encourage us to trust that silence, beginning with the psalmist's "be still and know that I am God" (Ps. 46:10). Being still before God is the enduring stance of prayer, that which lasts when all the words and other sounds inside are exhausted. The Latin word for listen, *obidare,* literally means "to obey." Being still inside is the purest form of listening, vulnerably listening for God through the silence.

We tend to treat silence and sound as different categories of reality, but I think they really are very intimate. In fact we might say that silence contains the full potential of sound. Sound seems really to emerge out of the silence not as a totally separate "thing," but as a particular *shaping* of the silence. Thus the sound in a sense is made of the silence; it is a particular expression of the silence, a specific coloring of it. Sound therefore retains a quality of silence. We might say that every sound has pure silence still present at its center. Insofar as we are particular sustained sounds of God, we ourselves share this same spacious, silent core. Thus sound need not take us away from silence, nor silence take us away from sound. We do not have to get away fully from one in order to touch the other. They appear to be warp and woof of the same reality.

If this closeness of sound and silence is true, it has important implications for the way we turn to God. God appears to be equally close to us through sound and silence. God is incarnate in creation as the deepest silent-hearted Sound. The Holy One is at the deep center of our own sound and silence.

So we turn to God through sound and silence as we would turn our heads to the left and the right, knowing that both directions reveal the same Heart, silently beating closer to us than our own hearts. Life in God is that intimate, and for this very reason that threatening to our confused egos which so identify ourselves as *ultimately* separate beings. We can take God as distant object but to accept God as intimate *subject* of our lives takes a revolution of grace, radically altering our sense of identity. Yet we can prepare for that revolution, or if it has already taken place, we can cultivate its seepage into all dimensions of our life. That is the process of sanctification, of ever fuller conversion of life.

EXERCISE 4: PRESENCE THROUGH SOUND AND SILENCE

This exercise is meant to help you with the very practical problem of distraction when you are intending a recollected presence to God. How can you let sound draw you toward such recollection rather than scatter your mind and feelings? Let's look carefully at how this scattering happens.

When you first hear a sound, for an instant it is just an open vibration from which you are not yet separated. Then one or both of two things occur: (a) You step outside the sound with your mind and give a *label* to it: "That is a mockingbird singing"; (b) You step outside the sound and *judge* it: "I don't like (or I do like) that sound."

This mental activity happens so rapidly that you usually do not even notice the sound before you have split off from it with an interpretation. However, if you let yourself hear the sound simply as a vibration without labeling or judging it (including not labeling it as "vibration"), you will remain *in* the sound. Then it is not a distraction that carries you away, but an experience of expansive awareness. Instead of being a distraction, the sound has a way of helping your presence. Since your mind is not "stopping" the sound, the sound has a way of washing through you, sometimes taking with it any busyness or heaviness inside.

When you notice that you have already fallen into labeling or judging a sound, you can gently return to an open presence. It might be helpful to sense the silence that remains in the middle of the sound and behind it, letting yourself remain still in that silence. Tell yourself that it is not necessary to make anything "extra" out of the sound during meditation. It is just simply vibration that need not divide your mind.

Besides the sounds you hear there are those that are shaped through you: the sounds you make. You can simply remain inside these sounds as well. This is easiest when chanting a very simple word or phrase. Let the sound rise easily through a relaxed throat. Let the vibration fill your whole body and mind with nothing left over, not even an observer, if possible. Anytime you notice something in you separating from the sound, gently rejoin it, so that there is nothing but the sound.

When you have chanted together (if in a group) for a while, the leader can clap or ring a bell, which calls the group to total silence. Identify with the silence now just as fully as you did with the sound. Let any sound simply be absorbed into the still openness of your mind. If your mind is moved, gently return to the silent center of the sound. (If you are alone, you also can chant for a while and then, as you feel ready, stop and identify with the silence.)

The normal curiosity, paranoia, and habits of your mind can make this exercise difficult. Noticing these aspects of the mind taking you away is valuable learning in itself, though. You begin to see more precisely some of the ways you are willingly or unconsciously distracted. The mind is a stubborn gift. Those searching functions of the mind that can be valuable at other times do not easily let go now when they need to. Instead of judging ourselves harshly, though, or even giving up in despair, it is best to smile gently and acceptingly through what you see happening, and let that smile draw you closer to a still, open presence once again.

You need to keep your underlying intent firmly before you: to drop through your scattered mind in sound and silence to a vulnerable, recollected presence for God. That purpose is both an end-in-itself being with God, and also a hope that God will secretly work in you through your vulnerable available presence for whatever might be needed: healing, compassion, repentance in the face of God's love, trust, and so on. Such firm intent is a sharp sword that can cut through the tangled meanderings of your mind and leave you more malleable in God's hands.

What chants can best serve this intent? Four normal criteria for selecting these are worth noticing. First, the chant should be *short* so that you are not distracted by trying to remember too much. Second, it should be *simple*, either monotoned or with very little variation in tone. This will allow easier participation by those who feel they cannot sing. One helpful thing about a simple chant is that everyone can do it, unlike more complicated singing. Third, it should include *resonant* words, ones that allow full-throated, open vowels. Finally, it should include a spiritually meaningful and powerful word. I particularly recommend the use of one of the names of God in Hebrew or Aramaic, such as *Adonai* ("Lord"), *Abba ("Father")*, *Amma* ("Mother"), *Yeshuah* ("Jesus: 'God saves' "), *Emmanuel* ("God with us"), or *Yahweh*.

This last name, *Yahweh*, is particularly symbolic for contemplative prayer, since it is really an acronym for the most intimate yet most vast and untranslatable name of God: "I am who I am" (Exod. 3:14). God is personally revealed to Moses, yet the "who" is both too close and too far to be captured by a proper name. Because of this, it is forbidden to be pronounced or written in Orthodox Jewish tradition. Jesus gave Christians a certain boldness in approaching God in prayer, and yet I think even Christians should dare use "Yahweh" only if they are open to its mysterious depth. Using it can encourage your mind to be vastly intimate, reflecting the image of God in which we are made.

The invocation of God's name has great power in Judeo-Christian tradition. To invoke the name is to call out for God's real presence here now. The names of God often come out more resonantly in Hebraic, Latin, or other languages. A non-English word also has the advantage of a little greater sense of mystery, a little less overfamiliarity.

Invocation of the name of Jesus in prayer is advocated in Scripture (e.g., John 15:16, Col. 3:17) and has a long history. Chanting the familiar English name of Jesus may be best for many people, but it is worth considering the use of the Hebrew-derived *Yeshuah* (or the Latin *Jesu*) for Jesus; this is very resonant and can be a fresh way into Jesus' presence. His name has been so overdomesticated in some Christian circles that its greatness can easily be lost. It is important to remember that when we chant his name we are not just addressing the historical person of Jesus, but the eternally living Logos, the redeeming personal presence of God incarnate in Jesus. We see this awareness in Jesus' own sense of identity when he said, "Before Abraham was, I am" (John 8:58). Such an identity also connects him to the great "I am" of Exodus 3:14: *Yahweh*.

Other good one-word chants besides the names of God include "shalom," "holy," "amen," and "alleluia." Short multiword chants also can be used; the psalms are particularly good sources for these. Sometimes the chant can be simplified to a single syllable, such as "om," or "ah," when you want to concentrate on the vibration rather than the meaning of the sound as a way of opening to God.

It is interesting to note the integration of the vibration and the meaning in the historic plainsong chanting of the Psalms. The sense of presence during such chanting usually is quite different than when the words are simply spoken. The chanting can draw the words deeper than their cognitive meanings, emptying you into a loving, recollected presence. When these are chanted in contemplative communities they reflect the whole rhythm of life cultivated there: words and physical acts constantly pour into a rich silence, out of which comes another round of words and acts. In such a way sounds and silence grow out of one another, a subtle dance through which God weaves a community of love, forgiveness, creativity, labor, and commitment to be present to the Presence through it all. These usually are struggling human communities like others, yet their rhythm of life, honed through centuries of testing, has much to teach all human communities.

This is a proposed sequence for the exercise.

1. Pray for your openness to God's presence through sound and silence.

2. Chant one of the words suggested (or some other word(s) that seem central to your relationship with God). Let yourself be fully in the sound with the full energy of your yearning for God, for at least ten minutes, preferably twenty.

The chant in a group can be sung in one of three ways. The first involves a *continuous* sound, i.e., everyone begins and ends the word when they are ready so that *among* everyone the sound is continuous. This will work well only if a single word chant is being used. It has the advantage of giving everyone an opportunity to chant at a pace natural for them. Its disadvantage is the awkwardness that beginners might feel. The second possibility is chanting in rhythm together. The third is singing antiphonally, or responsively with a leader.

3. Now be in *silence* as fully as you were in sound. Let every sound that registers simply expand the silence that never leaves. Just be present for God through a still, spacious, innocent mind. This should continue also for a minimum of ten, or preferably twenty minutes or longer, if the group is more experienced with silence.

REFLECTION QUESTIONS

After the exercise you can reflect on one or more of a number of questions.

1. Was there anything that seemed to be particularly graced (i.e., gifted from God) in your experience? This may be only a vague sense of something dawning, something on the edge of your awareness, and not easily articulated. Why would you call this "graced"?

2. Do you remember different qualities of awareness such as (a) being inside, not separate from, the sound and silence and being calm, clear, and energetic, (b) being outside them: observing, grasping, judging, agitated, having a sense of restricted awareness, or (c) being just dull, cloudy, in a low energy state?

3. Do you remember any sense of deeper presence, for example, through surrendering to God or being taken into the depth of

sound or silence in God? If so, what did this do to your sense of God and self?

4. Did you have any sense of "cleansing" taking place, i.e., of being washed, opened, or healed?

Reflection on such questions can help you begin to notice more carefully what is and can be happening in our awareness, including the movements of God's Spirit in us.

EXERCISE 5: PRESENCE THROUGH A WORD: A VERSION OF RECEPTIVE CENTERING PRAYER

Among a number of other possible exercises related to sound and silence I would like to single out just one more here. It involves the use of one of our faintest sounds: the vibration of a thought. Though it probably has never occurred to you to think of a thought as a sound, this indeed is true, and a thought can be a very powerful little sound indeed. Thoughts will be dealt with in a more precise way when we come to exercise 8. Here we will deal with a very particular thought word that, as an instrument of our will for God, can help lead us not to further thoughts, but to wordless presence for God.

The form of such contemplative prayer has many historical and contemporary variations, ranging from the Jesus Prayer to Centering Prayer. All of them share the same ultimate intent, though: the use of a word or phrase that symbolizes our will's consent to God's liberating presence.

These forms can be taught with different emphases, however. I will mention two. First, the Jesus Prayer, and related mantra-like prayer forms being taught today,[1] tend to emphasize the importance of silently repeating a prayer word or phrase extensively. Concentration on the word is important, even when the mind might otherwise seem still, until our hearts so fully rest in God that the word is finally taken away and we cannot say it any longer. This is a graced occurrence that we cannot force and should not willfully expect, but for which we can humbly hope.

The second form is modern Centering Prayer, as espoused by Thomas Keating, Basil Pennington, and others,[2] which draws on a contemplative tradition that includes the anonymous *Cloud of Unknowing* and the last contemplative stage of historic scriptural *lectio divina*. This strand of practice emphasises the cultivation of an open, receptive, lovingly attentive presence for God, using the word or phrase as a symbol of the will's intent for this presence. Instead of continuing to recite the word when the mind is still, it is dropped into the silence, to return only when the mind loses its immediate receptivity to God.

One value of the *first* way, as the Benedictine John Main once told me, is its capacity to bring us through quiet but cloudy, floating periods of the mind, toward a more clear presence for God. A value of the *latter* way, as Thomas Keating has said, is its capacity to open the unconscious more easily and allow a simple release of psychic debris that can come between us and God.

I have taught and practiced a modified version of this second, more receptive form of contemplative prayer for many years. As I describe it here, remember that it need not be practiced or taught in any single way. As you become experienced with it, you might find that it takes on its own unique way with you. Prayer is shaped by our personalities and by God in a slightly different way with each of us. Thus prayer forms, even historic ones, are not meant to be imitated mindless of your particular responsiveness. The forms we learn from others are tested ways of getting us started. How they evolve from there is an experiment we can predict only in broad strokes. One value of a spiritual director is having someone with whom we can note this distinctive evolution of the Spirit in our prayer and reflect together on the best way of letting it be carried forward.

PRAYER STEPS

1. Offer a simple prayer of desire to live into your liberating, calm depth in God, to go through everything to its open source in God, to let all that comes go to God, and thus share the mind of Christ.

2. Take several long, slow breaths. For several moments simply notice the contents of your mind. Begin to loosen your identification with them; don't treat them as your thought-possessions, but rather as simple appearances with which you do not personally identify, or latch onto, in a way that takes you away from an open presence. Gently let the contained thoughts, images, sounds, and feelings pass by without dwelling on any of them.

3. Let a short word rise from deep in the center of your being that is a resonant symbol of your desire for God's presence, a word that expresses your willingness to open into that presence. Don't try to force the word to come. Just listen for it with a relaxed, inviting, open mind.

4. Once a word has come, for the next twenty to thirty minutes (depending on your experience with silence) let your intent be to effortlessly fall through that word into God's spacious, wordless, uniting presence. Remain very still there, at the open source of your mind, willing to relinquish all the passing contents to God's cleansing, loving, illuminating radiance. If anything rises that takes away your still presence at the bottom of the parade of thoughts and images (or of your imageless presence), then very gently let the word return. Let the word be so full of calm, confident intent for God that any disturbance is simply melted into its spacious center. Seek nothing during this time except steadying, trusting, attentive rest in God. This is a time of sim-

ple, willing being in God's pervasive, loving presence. In its fullness, there is no reflective sense of self left at all (which would only be another thought), just a unitive awareness with neither subject nor object: everything simply *is*, in God. Part of our spiritual birthright is this end-in-itself, unreflective communing. (If you are leading a group into this prayer, I would suggest selecting only part of this description, or rewording it in your own succinct way, in order to keep it simple).

5. Return gently to your normal consciousness through use of some simple active words of thanksgiving or praise. This can be a spontaneous phrase of the moment, or a more standardized one such as the Gloria Patri or a longer prayer like the Lord's Prayer said slowly. I often will say a personalized form of the Gloria Patri: "Glory to you who create us, redeem us, and live in our hearts, now and forever." Then let your intent be to draw the fruits of your willingness for God's presence and whatever may have happened during the silence into the conceptual, feeling, and action dimensions of your life.

Such a simple, contemplative prayer form joined with your right intent can have an amazing capacity to draw you to deep awareness in God. This awareness is not cut off from other things, but rather is far more inclusive and connecting of everything than your more ordinary active consciousness, simply because you no longer are chopping reality into pieces with your mind. In the process of this prayer over time, you also can notice what a fine conditioning it provides for loosening your attachments. All those many thoughts, images, and feelings that you might normally allow to kidnap your attention are simply released to God during this prayer. The often confused, constrictive, grasping identity of your ego-self is relativized to a deeper identity grounded in God.

The result later on can be a mind more free to discern what is truly called for in terms of action or nonaction in life. I will return to this form of prayer in the chapter on acting in the world, because it can have value in the world directly, as well as more remotely through its use during an unambiguous period of prayer. Such special Centering Prayer time is an excellent daily practice. If it is practiced twice a day, more opportunity is given for its quality of presence to develop. The more easily we find ourselves drawn away from willingness for God's presence during the day, the more important it is to have a second period for such prayer.

For further practical elaboration of this kind of prayer, I would refer you to the books listed in note 2 for this chapter.

REFLECTION QUESTIONS

1. What was the impact of the word and your willingness for God within it on your quality of presence?

2. Were there times of fear where you pulled out of the stillness in distrust, fearing a loss of control by your "little self," or a related desire to produce or possess something with your mind, fearing a loss of your normal personal sense of reality and identification with what your mind produces or can grasp?

3. Did you have any inkling of your own and God's reality beyond your ego control and your mind's imaging—a sense of mutual presence in the spaces between these mental activities?

4. *If you have been using this kind of prayer for a while,* have you noticed any change in your word? (Over time the word might spontaneously shift to one that feels like a more "true" expression of your openness for the mystery of God's presence, but do not restlessly *try* for new words. The first one may be permanently right, or it may simplify itself to just a syllable. Eventually the word may be replaced by the quality of willing attentiveness that infuses the word, while the word itself falls away.)

5. Is there some other form of prayer that opens your presence for God in this way?

To return this centering prayer to our context of sound and silence, we might say that full contemplative prayer involves opening our narrowing sounds into God's inclusive Sound, and letting that Sound live through us, freeing, guiding, empowering us beyond our imagination. Contemplative prayer invites a quiet, hollow mind that does not stop sounds, but lets them draw us to God through the deep silence out of which they are shaped. Through the silence *and* the sound we can trust our unity with God, a unity that is always there before our minds pull away. The deepest sound and silence of God takes us into our spiritual heart, where we realize this unity in diversity most fully.

CHAPTER 4

Seeing

"...Who is it that sees behind the eye?" That is the rest of that verse from the Upanishads that I began in the last chapter (page 34). Jesus in effect challenges us to pay close attention to our answer when he speaks of our needing eyes that really see.[1]

Christian spiritual tradition reinforces this in what came to be called "custody of the eyes," which is still found in the rules of some religious communities. In its distorted form this practice came to involve a repressive, fearful, exaggerated attempt to exclude from sight all that might tempt one to sin. But in its authentic intent to assist recollection we are brought back to those ancient challenges: Who sees? How can we really see?

Let's look at three ways of seeing, which I shall call innocent, split, and participative.

Innocent Seeing. When we open our eyes to look, just as when we open our ears to hear, there is an instant before we separate from what we see in order to interpret it with our minds. We are just present *in* what we see, with an open innocence. Perhaps this is related to the quality of presence that Jesus meant when he said, "Whoever does not accept the kingdom of God as a child will not enter it" (Luke 8:17). A young child seems to stay in this innocent "first sight" longer than older people. In Matthew's version of this saying Jesus adds, "Whoever *humbles* himself like this child" (18:4). The Hebrew word for the Greek New Testament word used here appears to be the same one translated in Proverbs 9:4 as "simple" (RSV) or "ignorant" (JB): "Whoever is simple [ignorant], let him step this way." A small child's humility is simple, without pretense; ignorant, without self-consciousness.

Split Seeing. The innocent flash fades as our minds step outside the unity in order to see through the mind's interpretive power. As this happens a hard object is created, split off from a subject (the interpreting mind). Self-consciousness rises with this split. Desires rise in concert with this sense of separateness: to reach out and possess in word or fact what we no longer are part of, or to protect what now feels vulnerably separate (we will return to this phenomenon when we deal with self-image).

This capacity to relate analytically to our environment is a marvelous gift. Most of our societal training cultivates it. The good fruits include our enormous power to manipulate what we see with our analytical comprehension and bend it toward our scientific and moral will. The bitter fruit is the tendency of this way of seeing to imperially define itself as the only valid way of seeing. As I brought out in a previous book, this way of seeing has almost totally eclipsed the participative, contemplative way of seeing (and thus, knowing) that was widely affirmed in the Church prior to the sixteenth century (with some exceptions since then in the realm of the arts and continuing contemplative traditions).[2]

Participative Seeing. Participative seeing marks the beginning of contemplative awareness. It involves a way of remaining innocently present with our eyes (just as we do with our ears), adding to the pure innocent way of seeing an intentional quality of energetic awareness. In this awareness we can desire to live directly out of God's vibrant presence.

Such participative seeing qualifies our understanding of analytical sight. The latter takes place within a still coinherent reality; its outsideness is relative to this reality. This being so, it is possible to see analytically without finally separating from either the situation or God. However, our confused, willful egos easily bury this reality and we then find this spiritual eye blinded, leaving our sight controlled by our grasping, protecting, split-off little-self consciousness.

"No one has ever seen God" (John 1:18), that is, as an object. Jesus says we can in a sense see God with our spiritual eye: "Blessed are the pure in heart [the single-hearted], for they shall see God" (Matt. 5:8). The pure in heart see without guile or pretense, without ultimate self-conscious protection or assertion. They desire with their whole being to see life whole in God. After death, this seeing hopefully will be brought to its fullness.

The single-hearted have "the single eye" that Jesus says is necessary if we are to be a body of light rather than of darkness (Matt. 6:22). This is a single, whole eye, not a double eye; it is an eye that is willing and graced to be more one, than two, with God, an eye through which God sees. Meister Eckhart said, "The eye with which I see God is the same eye with which God sees me".[3] That is very intimate indeed: the unity in diversity that marks spiritual union.

ICONS

A graced eye at its fullest is a gift of God. And yet we can dispose ourselves for this grace of sight, just as we can with sound. I want to hold up one classical and powerful means for conditioning this participative eye, a means that potentially opens all sights as transparencies of the divine: the practice of sitting (or standing) before holy icons. I have touched on this subject in past writings. Now I would like to take it further, both in providing more background and by including a concrete way of being present to God through icons.

Apart from the cross and the Gospels, and encounters with spirit-filled people, perhaps nothing conditioned the Christian spiritual eye in the first millennium of the Church as much as holy icons; and the importance of icons continues to this day especially in the Eastern Orthodox churches. Indeed, the cross, the Gospels, and icons are mentioned in the same breath in the declaration of the Seventh Ecumenical Council (in the year 787). All three are placed on an equal level for veneration. Long before then, St. Basil declared these painted images of Jesus, Mary, and other biblical and saintly figures to be equal to Scripture in their capacity to reveal God's presence.

But how can we venerate images in the face of the Second Commandment: "You shall not make for yourself a graven image, or any likeness of anything that is in heaven above, earth beneath, or that is in the water under the earth; you shall not bow down to them or serve them" (Exod. 20:4–5)?

This is an ancient question. Those who said you cannot venerate images were the people who participated in the destruction of icons during the great iconoclastic controversies of the eighth and ninth centuries, just as Puritans destroyed religious objects, even crosses, in the sixteenth century. But the weight of historical Eastern Orthodox, Anglican, and Roman Catholic tradition (as well as the witness of the early church) has come down on the side of the formal use of images, taking great care in drawing the line between veneration that assists our awareness of God, and worship that creates idols.

Indeed, when this distinction is carefully made, there may be no need for ultimate conflict between the inheritors of Puritan tradition and others, since the venerated images would be "purified" of idolatry. Images in the broad sense of relating what we see to God are an inescapable dimension of spiritual life. The question is how to do this without *replacing* God by what is seen. Authentic religious images have provided a vital way of training the contemplative eye and human affections and of concentrating the will. They provide an infinite subject worthy of the infinite longing within us (compared to the finite subjects of contemporary commercial and political images). They need to be complemented by the great Reformation reaffirmation of biblical and interpretive language (*verbal* images) as a way to God's presence. We need not have to choose between image and language in the emerging great church of our time, though. *Both* are needed if our means of formation are not to be impoverished.[4]

No artistic pictorial tradition has been more careful, profound, and grounded in the Church's teaching in its way of approaching God than that of holy icons. Sacred icons are rooted in the Incarnation. God sounds the eternal Word into a human form. In Jesus, God is mysteriously shown; he is an *icon* (the Greek work for "image") of God, "not made with human hands" (Heb. 9:11). In the legendary origin of the sacred icons of Jesus' face, the king of Edessa receives a gift of that face imprinted on a cloth, an image "not made with human hands." (Some interpretations of the Shroud of Turin and Veronica's Veil may be related to this same tradition.) In tracing icons of Jesus to this origin, they become rooted not in the autonomous imagination of some artist, but in a gift from Jesus himself.

Another affirmation of icons came from John Damascene in the early Church when he said that Jesus was born not just of a nonrepresentative Father, but of a representative Mother. This allows us to portray both Mother and Son (though never the "Father").

More deeply than these reasons, though, lies a sense that God's intimacy in the Incarnation frees us to utilize the intimacy of a painting to carry forward such an awareness of God's indwelling presence among us. In Christ God reveals the called-for unity of image and Spirit, which in turn frees us to do likewise. Yet it cannot be just any painting. It needs to carry the authentic revelation of God as agreed upon by the early Church. This led over time to certain guidelines for sacred icons.

1. Like the Incarnation itself, such paintings need to reflect a deep spiritual reality "not made with human hands." Thus the painting should not emerge from the artist's subjective ego. Rather, through a process of prayer, fasting, and sometimes spiritual direction, the painting emerges out of the artist's firsthand contemplation and knowledge of the gospel. The icon thus is not a personal creation, but a description of what is contemplated, an in-touchness with the mysterious truth of the tradition.[5]

2. In order to assure its continuity with the truth of the tradition, it must be painted in a style that reflects the tradition. This requires the artist to listen deeply to the Holy Spirit's expression in existing icons and draw upon this same Spirit in his or her icon. Good craftmanship is not sufficient for this. It is not a matter of imitation, but of the artist's interiorized spiritual knowledge of "God becoming human, so that we might become God," as St. Athanasius put it in the early Church. Thus the artist is showing forth the transfigured human state to which we are called, the body's participation in divine life. The artist is charged with portraying this Good News in a way that draws all our faculties into its realization.

3. This process is assisted by requiring that the icon technically be two-dimensional. Three dimensions (as in a statue) would tempt focus on the particular isolated human form, just as too personal a rendition

might. It needs to be more of a transparency for reality in God, not a form that draws attention to itself.

In another sense Byzantine-influenced icons are three-dimensional. They have a reverse perspective where the vanishing point is in effect behind the viewer rather than in the icon. The viewer thereby is drawn into the icon and becomes related to it. This method emphasizes the *participative* quality of knowledge in contemplative tradition, as opposed to an objective, outside observing, analytical way of knowing, which has never been sufficient for realizing spiritual truth. The transfigured spirit-body integration of an icon can be authentically appreciated only through faithful participation in its enlivening spirit.

4. The highly stylized form also is meant to assist the icon's transparency for reality in God. The form is not meant to be "inhuman," but just the reverse. It is meant to show us our fullest humanity illuminated in the Spirit, a transfigured state of body and spirit incomprehensibly comingled.

In older Byzantine-influenced icons that include a number of people and buildings, these forms are often painted without background perspective or logical placement. This method also can reflect the same sense of reality in the Spirit. The promised fullness of God's presence as seen in the transfigured state is being portrayed. That fullness does not conform to our normal human ways of seeing reality. The merging of foreground and background, for example, becomes a way of confounding our logic and inviting us deeper.

5. The icon is meant to complement other means of exposing the gospel. As St. Basil put it, "What the word transmits through the ear, the painting silently shows through the image . . .by these two means, mutually accompanying one another . . .we receive knowledge of one and the same thing."[6] Thus, as Leonid Ouspensky puts it, the icon has the same mystic, liturgic, and educational significance as Scripture.

The written and painted word are exposed together in the Eastern Orthodox Divine Liturgy, which enacts what the icons show and the words say. Thus action, word, and image are brought together as reinforcing dimensions of a single liturgical whole. This powerful public function of icons guides their subject matter, focusing them on significant biblical revelatory events and people, as well as certain later saints of particular significance to the Church.

In the Eastern Orthodox world icons are placed everywhere, in homes, churches, public places, and pockets, "as revelation of the future sanctification of the world and its coming transfiguration, as pattern of its realization, and as promulgation of grace and presence."[7] It is important to realize how pervasive the sense of divine presence is in Orthodox tradition. The saints portrayed in icons are part of this presence. The communion of saints is a living reality. The saints live and intercede for us. The icons participate in the living divine energies of those portrayed. It is of course hard for the self-centered human ego not to turn any sign of the sacred into an opportunity for personal oversecuring and aggrandizement. But icons are too precious a means of teaching, prayer, and presence to throw out just because they can fall prey to misuse.

The use of icons has long been valued in various branches of the Western Church as well. In many Western churches three-dimensional statues and crosses have been mixed in with a great variety of two-dimensional art forms, all accepted as part of the church's spiritual life, but these have not been so integrally woven into the heart of Western theology and related public practice as in the Eastern Church.

What kind of icon is best for use in long meditation? There is no one right answer to that. However, I can offer a few suggestions out of my experience.

1. The icon should have a capacity to draw you into the mystery of God's Spirit illumining human form.

2. This will likely be more obvious in an icon with only one or two figures, probably one of Jesus or of Jesus and Mary (unless you have a background of relationship with particular saints). The eyes of one or more of these sacred personages should be particularly apparent, and looking directly toward you.

3. A pre–seventeenth-century icon, or a later one that is clearly made with the intent and style of such an early icon, will probably be best. A certain corruption by earlier standards becomes apparent beginning with particular seventeenth-century icons, in which they lose their testimony to the transfigured state. As Ouspensky notes, "One can distort the teaching of the Church by image as well as by word."[8]

Both personally and in groups I have used two particular icons. One is of the Risen Christ, commissioned for Shalem by one of our participants. It is based on one of my favorite contemporary icons (in turn based on an older style) that I once found in a small chapel in the restored Church of the Multiplication of the Loaves at Tabgha on the edge of the Sea of Galilee. As in all such figures of Christ I know of, the Greek words o φν, literally "The Being," surround the head. These I am told derive from Exodus 3:14, the revelation of God's mysterious name to Moses. For me they help guard the image from idolatry. God the Creator can never be portrayed in an authentic Eastern Orthodox icon. The Christ rises out of this background as an image of the Imageless One. The intimate image is kept in the perspective of the vastness of God. I am led through the intimacy of the image into the great spaciousness of God, and at the same time I realize God coming through Christ to me, wanting to free my image to reflect the divine image in which I was made.

The other icon I frequently use is a copy of the great twelfth century "Our Lady of Vladimir,"[9] painted in Constantinople, but transferred to Russia, where it has continued to be one of the most venerated of icons. Mary's eyes have a way of drawing me toward deep, cleansing compunction and compassion. Indeed, this icon is in the school of "icons of loving kindness," which depict mutual gestures of loving kindness between Mary and the child Jesus, while at the same time Mary's eyes seem inwardly turned toward the full Mystery of God.

Isaac of Syria, in the early Church, said that the sign of a fully merciful heart is present when it "burns for all creation." You can sense this integrally human-divine mercy in Mary's eyes. It is not in the least a sentimental emotion (i.e., a kind of cloudy, oversecuring, ego level, sweet "high") that is evoked. Rather it evokes a deep, raw, honest sensing of human life as it is in God's eyes, including life in all its deception, suffering, and willfulness, and yet penetrated by the proferred, empowering love of God.

Mary is not a personally intimate sacred figure to most Protestants, who have not been raised in those traditions where weight is given to her continuing relationship with us. Today, though, she has been coming to the fore more ecumenically as an invaluable exemplar of trusting responsiveness to God. Through Mary's consent God emerged in our midst in fresh form. She is in a sense mother of our trust and our hope for fullness. Mary, the *Theotokos* ("God-bearer"), models the way our very being is called to birth the love, creativity, and bearing joy of the One who births us. In this sense we all become mothers of God.

Such attending of God through Mary has the special value of giving us a feminine sacred image through which to approach God. I feel sure that God intends us to be free to pass through both divinely proferred feminine and masculine images, into the full transpersonal Holy Presence.

With this background on icons, let me offer now a way of being present to God through them, remembering that it is not the only way. As I shall encourage in the homework section, attention to a particular holy icon can sensitize us to letting everything we see become a potential icon of God. Then all that we see can draw us toward God rather than away from God.

EXERCISE 6: PRAYING THROUGH AN ICON

These steps are worded for group leaders; but they can easily be adapted for individuals praying alone:

1. Offer enough background (in written or oral form) about icons to help people understand their spiritual value. Then light a candle before the icon as a symbol of the living divine presence. If the group is large you might want to have two icons available, perhaps a Christ

icon and one of the Blessed Virgin and Child. The larger in size the icons are, the better. If it is a very large group, a projected slide of an icon can be used. Give people several moments to stand very close to the icon first (unless it is a slide), especially encouraging them to look into the eyes. If there is a choice of icons, this is the time for everyone to sense which one seems best for them to sit before.

2. Ask everyone to sit as close to the icon as space allows, without blocking others' view.

3. Ask everyone to close their eyes and offer a prayer that expresses their desire to touch God's presence through the icon, and to relinquish whatever may distance them from that intent. A short, simple chant might also be included here to assist their presence. For example, if they are before an icon with Mary they might chant the first line of the Magnificat in the first chapter of Luke: "My soul magnifies the Lord"; if they are with an icon of the Christ, they might chant his name in some form, such as the Aramaic *Yeshuah*.

4. Now these suggestions can be made: "Open your eyes and look at the eyes of the icon. Spend a moment reaching for God with your will through the eyes. Resist the normal impulse to grasp for some kind of knowledge, instead, keeping your eyes very still, and letting *yourself* be *known* by God through the icon's eyes. Gently release any sense of judgment, distance, hardness, curiosity, or distrust as these may arise."

Optional. Some of the following suggestions can also be made to the group.

"Let yourself be hollowed out so that you might become aware of God's gaze through the eyes of the icon seeing through all that you are with severe love. Let nothing remain hidden or outside this receptive exposure. Open space for the One who loves you through and through, and let yourself be open for whatever secret cleansing, healing, or illumining might come.

"Seek to let this 'being known' by God so fill your knowing that you are left with a mutual knowing that is beyond a hard subject-object relationship. Move close to that mind of innocent seeing, of coinherent presence. There is nothing to think about, just a quality of still, open, naked being, a descent to the single eye of your heart."

If you are leading a group, you need to be very selective about what (if anything) you suggest from this optional section. It is important not to overprescribe people's experience with too many leading suggestions. Keep it simple. I have given more description than needed here in order to familiarize you with some possibilities of prayer with an icon.

Have the group spend twenty to thirty minutes for this step (it is important that you sense the Spirit's timing in such a potentially powerful practice).

5. When step 4 is completed, suggest the following: "Close your eyes, trying to retain a sense of the icon in your mind. Then let it fade to a formless presence. Finally, try to sense the eyes of the icon re-appearing as *your* eyes, God seeing the world through you. Thus you may find yourself *becoming* the icon, realizing yourself to be an image of God, through whom the world is loved into the fullness of being."

This will probably have been the first time that most group members have ever prayed so intensively, if at all, with an icon. It is particularly good to give everyone at least one or two further opportunities to be with the icon, so that it might become less strange and more natural for them. If you are on a residential retreat, it can be particularly good to have one or more icons where they can remain visible, and people can return to them as they are moved.

REFLECTION QUESTIONS

1. What was it like to try and let yourself be "known" by God through the icon? (e.g., how much trust and openness were present, and how much fear and resistance?)
2. What was the effect of the eyes of the icon becoming your eyes, if this happened for you?
3. Was there any seemingly graced moment that revealed something crucial for your way of seeing and being?
4. Can you think of any painting or other object that has been a special icon of God for you in the past?

Homework. The days following this practice can be a crucial time for translating it into ongoing prayerful awareness with your eyes. Some people may have an opportunity to pray before a classical icon. Even without one, though, people might find it possible to bring the icon back in their imagination and sit before it, so to speak.

Beyond this, everyone can be asked to let every visible sight potentially become an icon for them: Practice letting yourself be "known" by God through whatever you see, instead of always putting your effort into a grasping kind of knowledge. Let your eye be still, your mind innocently open, as you drop through your normal way of being present to people, trees, stones, etc., and sense them as latent transparencies for God.

Thus any way you turn, God is there knowing you and the situation. You are there available to that Presence, letting it inform, or better transform, your awareness and action. Just as with sound and movement, there is no way your sight can turn away from God, unless your mind pulls you away out of blindness or willfulness. God's eye and your eye are that close.

The following quotations are scriptural references, one or more of which you may be particularly moved to hold in your consciousness during the early days of your practice:

"You know me through and through." (Ps. 139:14, JB)
"We do not fix our gaze on what is seen but on what is unseen." (2 Cor. 4:18, NAB)
"My soul magnifies the Lord. . . ." (Mary's Song, the Magnificat, Luke 1:46ff)
"I know my own and my own know me, as the Father knows me and I know the Father." (John 10:14–15)

Alternative Exercises If classical icons do not seem an appropriate practice to take on, or if you want to follow them with other exercises related to seeing, one possibility is simply to focus on a candle flame, a bowl of water, a loaf of bread, a piece of crystal, or some other form. The steps of meditation suggested for icons, as well as the questions, homework, and scriptural suggestions, can be simplified and adapted for use with these.

EXERCISE 7: INTERIOR VISUALIZATION

Besides such exterior foci, you can add an interior visualization. One example is the visualization of light. Many New Testament phrases draw out the power of this symbol for God's radiant, loving truth, as well as its occasional physical manifestation when God's glory has a visible effect: "God is light" (1 John 1:5); "the glory of the Lord shone around them" (Luke 2:9); "[Jesus] is the light of the world" (John 8:12); his face and clothes were radiant (Matt. 17:2); "you are the light of the world" (Matt. 5:14); "walk as children of light" (Eph. 5:8); "the eye is the lamp of the body" (Matt. 6:22).

One of the ways light can be visualized is by closing your eyes and letting a bright, white star (or cross) of light emerge in the middle of your forehead, allowing it to become as still and three-dimensional as possible. If you have difficulty with such imaging (as many people do), you can simply sense that the light is there, feeling its warmth. Let this light stand for the light of Christ through which you are lovingly known, a light which gently absorbs all the thoughts and feelings that rise. Be very still and present to God through this time in your intent. The more still your mind, the more still the light will be.

The visualization can be preceded by a simple chant, such as the resonant Latin "Lumen Christi," the "Light of Christ" (which is chanted in procession during the Easter Vigil in many churches). Let it be a call for God's light that is in Christ to be realized in you.

This practice can be extended now or at another time by letting the light slowly expand throughout your body as an opening, cleansing light, and then beyond your body, so that within and without there is an even light of God. Your breathing in and out is filled with this light.

REFLECTION QUESTIONS

1. What was given you to let yourself be lovingly known through the light?
2. What personal experiences come to mind related to light, darkness, and God?

Homework. If you are leading a group, one or more of those "light" scriptural passages mentioned a few paragraphs back can be given for daily attention as well as the practice itself. Weight should be given more to *realizing* God's radiant light in and among us than to *analyzing* it. At the deepest, most graced, and rare level, such attention to interior light goes beyond symbolism, imagination, invitation, and awareness of ordinary presence to God. A quality of light can appear with surprising power, a possible indication of real Presence through which divine action occurs in some form, such as healing or deeper conversion. We may or may not be conscious of this divine action at the time.

QUESTIONING THE MIND: FROM SELF-IMAGE TO IDENTITY IN GOD

The practices mentioned thus far in this chapter aim at assisting the quality of "participative seeing" that I earlier described as basic to contemplative awareness. As I pointed out, our minds tend to quickly split away from such innocently aware presence in order to respond to the situation (analytically, emotionally, or in some other way). Even when we move toward a more participative presence, however, we usually find that there is still something left standing outside: a very subtle, at best semiconscious, defining sense of self.

If we close our eyes a moment we may be able to vaguely sense this self-image lurking beneath our awareness. When it is treated as an orienting sense of self that allows us to function in the world, it is a true and proper friend. However, this self-image normally is much more than this to us: it is not just an *image* of our self; we mistake it for our very self. Then it becomes something we feel the need to strongly protect, out of fear, or to enhance, out of a desire for its imperial expansion. Everything that rises to consciousness then is filtered according to its value to the self-image. At a more obvious level we can see this happening in such defense mechanisms as rationalization and projection, and in self-justifications of all kinds. What is being defended is the ultimate importance of this imaged sense of self.

When I look at a crucifix, it has the power of relaxing the ultimacy of such an ego-based self-image. The story of the Passion in one sense is the story of a variety of strong human self-images asserting and protecting themselves in the face of one who finally refused to define himself through such images. Instead, Jesus identifies himself (and us) ultimately in God's image, and beyond that even: in God beyond image. "I and the Father are one" (John 10:30). The world's strident self-images crumble on the cross. They cannot defeat the one who will not play their game. The hanging body, with its willing relinquishment of self-image's ultimacy, carries away the idolatrous power of self-image, for those who have eyes that really see.

When the ultimacy of self-image dissolves, what is left? Our great fear is that the answer is nothing, and on one level this answer is true. No thing is left standing between us and God, or between us and participation in God's creation. The "I" now is no longer a contained image which is ultimately defining and controlling. "I" now becomes infinitely larger and more open, but it is not an enlarged ego that "I" pridefully possess; rather, "I" becomes an expression of God's creative life that ultimately cannot be possessed. Such an "I" knows enormous freedom from the possessive, fearful, grasping ways of the "I" who was over identified with self-image.

If we press to the fullest St. Paul's plea for us to develop the self-emptying mind of Christ (Phil. 2:5), wherein not "I" but "he" lives in me (Gal. 2:20), we come to the same point. "Christ living in me" involves Jesus' self-awareness in God that lies behind his words, "Before Abraham was, I am." At the bottom of his identity, I believe, is this timeless vastness of God, who loves and shapes into existence the personal form and mission of Jesus, and lives within him in a unique way for us all. We are saved from the deadly ultimacy of a confined self-image when we let ourselves open to our Living Wellspring through the mind of Christ that we share in God's grace.

Once again, self-image is not destroyed in this process. Rather it becomes an expedient awareness, a reflective, practical sense of self, with a distinctive coloring and style deriving from our unique personhood. This self-image provides us with one way of relating to the world, and through (as well as beyond) it God loves and moves the world. But since we are free from confusing self-image with our ultimate identity in Christ, there is a certain playfulness rather than deadly seriousness in its functioning, a graced fluidity rather than self-focused rigidity.

Our identity on this functional level is full of little desires, fears, and resultant actions. When these are attacked, praised, accomplished, or frustrated, we can retain a certain lightness, because we know the relativity of our expedient self-image to our larger identity in God. This lightness, when shared with others, has enormous positive consequences for human living, as we shall see in later chapters.

EXERCISE 8: OPENING THOUGHTS TO GOD

The distinction between expedient self-image and our full self in God is not easy to grasp and infinitely more difficult to live out. It perhaps brings us here to the most subtle, challenging, and liberating awareness of life in God. The exercise I will now introduce is meant to provide you with an experiential opportunity to help realize what the concepts are pointing toward, though their full realization is in God's hands and timing.

I recommend this exercise (and exercise 9) for individuals and groups that are highly motivated toward careful contemplative practice. It involves an energetic, confident, willing, and precise attention of a more "spiritual psychological" nature. Its various steps can be spread out over a number of sessions: do not rush them. They can be very challenging and disorienting to our normal sense of reality and thus need time for absorption and integration into our awareness. Because of their unfamiliar kinds of demands on our attention I hesitated to include them in this book at all, but have done so because they are so revealing for some people. If you have trouble understanding this section of the book on subtle aspects of our consciousness, don't worry about it. It is not necessary for salvation! Some people will find relevant reading in this area to be helpful.[10] As with any of the exercises in this book, you need to discern whether or not you are truly drawn to this exercise now as an appropriate means of assisting your freedom for God. It should not be undertaken merely out of experimental curiosity, or out of any sense of necessity for your spiritual well-being.

This exercise begins by helping us watch the way our thoughts rise out of the innocent, undivided presence (described at the start of this chapter), moves toward a way of maintaining that participative presence, and finally attends the self-image and its "observer" that condition our presence.

1. Close your eyes and for about five minutes and count with numbers everything that registers in your mind: images, sounds, concepts, feelings, and "self-image consciousness" itself to the degree it separately registers. Do no try for thoughts. Just let your mind be the way it normally is, except instead of grasping after your thoughts, simply count them.

2. Close your eyes for another five minutes. Instead of noticing the thoughts this time, see if you can notice and stay in the space between and behind your thoughts. As any thought begins to rise, gently let it pass by without grabbing it. If you do notice yourself dwelling on a thought, gently let it go into the open spaciousness between thoughts.

3. Close your eyes once more. For a final period of ten minutes or longer, notice your thoughts again, but this time not as distinct ends

in themselves to count. Rather, see them as particular shapings of that spaciousness out of which they seem to rise (just as in exercise 4 you tried to notice sounds as shapings of the great inclusive silence). Thoughts then may be sensed as something like bubbles rising up, retaining their transparency and openness, their intimacy with the atmosphere out of which they appear. Through the desire of our faith in God's promised presence, this intimacy can extend to God, who pervades and sustains this matrix.

4. If Centering Prayer is known to you (see exercise 5), for ten minutes or longer return to doing this with your centering "word." Let your intent be for that word to open to God all your thoughts and the spaces between them. Thus you can hope to retain a certain evenness of presence to God through both thoughts and spaces.

5. Open yourself like a question mark to God. Listen for anything shaped for you that seems to come from God's liberating presence.

These first steps among other things can reinforce your capacity to let your identity be recollected in God through thoughts and spaces, rather than becoming narrowed down and split off by them. If the thoughts are being conditioned by an overpowerful ego self-image, you may be able to notice this and relinquish your overattachment to that image, freeing your deeper identity in God. Even if the power of your ego self-image is too great to avoid some attachment, something deeper in you knows that this is temporary and not final.

REFLECTION QUESTIONS

1. How did you experience the relation of the contents of your mind, their background spaciousness, and God?
2. Did you sense the freedom to sustain an evenness of presence to God through both the thoughts and spaces? What seemed to challenge this freedom?
3. Did anything come to you in step 5?

A provocative scriptural passage relevant to this and the next exercise is St. Paul's statement in 2 Corinthians 6:10: "having nothing, yet possessing all things." As applied here, it might draw out the paradox of possessing all things precisely because you are not attached to any one thing. You have not cut off one thing to privately possess and cling to, even your self-image. Rather, you are open to receive from God's infinite bounty all that rises without isolating possession, but with a stewardship that remains rooted in God. Your true richness is in God, who cannot be possessed in an ego sense.

Exercise 9 is best done at a later time if you are in a group, unless you are meeting together for a particularly long period. If you are only meeting weekly, exercise 8 needs at least a week or two to slowly settle into daily awareness. During those days you can continue to notice what is happening in your mind, and the way your identity in God may appear when your ego self-image loses its ultimacy.

EXERCISE 9: SUSPENDING THE INTERIOR OBSERVER

In this ninth exercise, I would ask you to focus on a subtle, seemingly sustained "thought" that conditions our presence constantly. I refer to it as the observer inside, the sense of a neutral or judging watcher, which in turn is born out of self-image. It is the *eye* of the self-image, that emerges into existence every time you step outside of your innocent participation in reality in order to do something to it.

When you try to experience your self-image, the observer is the first thing you encounter. Everything else about your experience of self-image tends to be only a vague sensing of some hidden, self-referring, conditioning power. So the observer becomes a very important connector to your sense of self. You will tend to identify with the observer as "me," in a more particular sense than with self-image in general.

As I touched upon earlier, ego self-image in its simplest dimension seems to be an expedient function of our real identity in God. It is insubstantial in itself, yet you will normally cling stubbornly to it as the ultimate "me." When it is in abeyance, your deeper awareness in God is activated, a participative awareness that cannot be threatened as your wobbly observer can be.

In that awareness you are open to "the peace that passes understanding." You are also open to receive authentic impulses for understanding and appropriately acting. Usually this open awareness is extremely brief, however; you quickly split off an observer in order to reflect and often try to possess, take credit for, and elaborate what is happening, instead of allowing simple stewardship that remains rooted in God.

I hope this will make more sense as you practice the following exercise.

1. Close your eyes and relax. Begin to notice your mind and a sense of something, of someone, doing the looking there. Once you are aware of this observer, with great energy look directly at the observer. If the observer dissolves, experience the pure, open, substantial, objectless state of your consciousness in the flash of the observer's disappearance and remain there as long as you can.

You might notice an observer of the observer has risen. If you do, look directly at this one, and any others that rise, so that you are continually returning to the innocent mind of pure awareness whenever possible. Do not judge the observers that rise, just notice and release, notice and release, with much alert energy, but with more of a sense of surrender than effort. Continue doing this for at least ten minutes.

2. After resting a few moments, return to noticing the observer. Where does the observer come from? Don't *think* about an answer, but try to directly *experience* where it comes from. Do this for at least ten minutes.

Now there can be some sharing of experience if you are in a group. No single answer to the question will be "right." All answers, if they are genuinely coming out of firsthand experience rather than conceptual guessing, will give probing words that describe some dimension of sensed ego need as source for the observer's recurrent birth.

I hope that through this exercise everyone will have sensed a reality to themselves that exists before the observer rises, a dawning sense that there is a quality of knowing, participative, living awareness present that does not require the commentary of an observer. In that awareness we are most directly involved in reality as it is. As I mentioned earlier, I believe that out of that awareness flows our most spontaneous and on-target seeing and doing.

We all have this awareness. We have all been influenced by it. I think it is God's clearest channel. But each observer is usually born too fast for us to notice it, and each observer has a tendency to skew what it sees toward the ego self-image's need to protect and expand its centrality. This centrality may simply involve conformity to familiar categories of understanding rather than anything particularly "selfish" in the moral sense.

I must reiterate once again that this ego self-image basically is a needed friend and not an enemy. But its confusion about its centrality, and a certain willful quality in us that can help keep it so, leads this flexible functional filter in us to become hardened into "the ultimate me." Its ultimate defense and assertion then leads to much of our personal and corporate woes. Its ultimacy lies behind what historically is called "our fallen nature," redeemed in Christ, but not yet fulfilled.

3. One more *related step* that can be done alone or in a group involves the use of a mirror. What happens to your awareness when you look into a mirror? St. Paul says that "we, with our unveiled faces reflecting like mirrors the brightness of the Lord, all grow brighter and brighter as we are turned into the image that we reflect; this is the work of the Lord who is Spirit" (2 Cor. 3:18, JB). Sitting in front of a mirror for half an hour, preferably a full hour at a time, can help condition our mind for its availability to the Spirit. Such availability among other things involves the lightening of our attachment to the ultimacy of ego self-image, and in the process freeing our deeper, more open identity rising out of God.

You might feel more secure if someone else knows you are doing this exercise, and if you can share what happens with them or another person afterwards. I say this in light of the disorienting, surprising, and revealing experience that may evolve.

Before beginning the process, seat yourself about two feet away from a mirror.

The Process. First pray for God's loving guidance through whatever comes. Desire to simply trust and surrender to God's presence through whatever comes. Then let the eyes you see in the mirror look into your eyes, rather than grasping for something in the mirror with your eyes. Just as with the icon exercise, let yourself be known through those eyes by God, but with no observer left defining out a "me," a "mirror image," or "God." Just let your mind be energetically stilled and opened through the gaze of the mirror icon.

Many phenomena may occur, including boredom, but allow yourself to settle into an even, confident-in-God awareness through whatever happens. If an observer appears, gently let it dissolve, or at least keep it very lightly on the fringes of your consciousness where it is more like a "glow" of awareness than an outsider.

Later you may sense how much your mind projected into the mirror, which is a vivid example of your insular ego image at work shaping the world to its own image. This may include dreamlike events, people, and things that seem vastly beyond your conscious concoction. Finally, you may be swept into a graced, unitive awareness that has a quality of a full, vibrant inclusiveness beyond any image; an awareness wherein there seems to be no barriers left between you and God's creation. Self-image is calmed. You no longer are relating an image of self to an image of creation, and an image of God, but rather real self, real creation, and real God are flowing together, experienced as the deepest sense of Home.

The mirror, in short, like a revealing crystal ball, has a way of rapidly showing you a myriad of productions of ego-self. As these are released, we give God room to reveal our true nature and unity as God may will to do so. The mirror can be a powerful, pregnant vehicle of spiritual awareness. Use it only when you are physically fresh and seem drawn to it, but be prepared for a certain internal resistance. Once again your confused friend, your insular sense of self, fears losing its control of your self-definition. But you are so much larger in God than it would have you believe. At the same time you are so much smaller in terms of anything that can be finally possessed in isolation from God. That is the great paradox of our human nature: made in the image of God, yet made of passing dust that has no ultimate substance of its own.

CHAPTER 5

Communing

Community: what everybody wants, but almost no one is able to sustain well for long.

In that succinct definition we find a great human dilemma! The old saw about the opposite sex puts it more bluntly: "You can't live with 'em, and you can't live without 'em." We can generalize this saying to the infinite varieties of attractions and differences that we face in community at all levels. What can a contemplative perspective bring to this dimension of living and spiritual formation?

Most fundamentally, it contributes the spiritual heart that experiences life as intrinsically coinherent. That heart realizes the "insideness" of things: everything is woven out of the same stuff of creation. A human being is a distinctive cross-sectional slice of that creation. Each of us is a unique shaping of the same great fertile silence and spaciousness of God, a particular expression of God's one love.

When we find ourselves in the quality of open awareness described in so many ways throughout this book, we at least taste the edge of this knowledge. There is no "outside" in the fullness of that awareness, but there is community. Everything is together and belongs.[1] Differences are seen, but these take the form of distinctive, vibrant transparencies rather than hard, boundaried, opaque things. There is a sense, or at least a trust, that the vibrant shapes are rising ultimately from the same Source: a Creator who both pervades this coinherent reality and yet is infinitely beyond it.

Theological descriptions of God in orthodox Christian tradition speak of the coinherence found in God's own nature, a Triune Unity, each Person lovingly flowing into the other without loss of distinctiveness, a dynamic diversity that is all "inside" one Beingness. Contemplative theologians are all those people whose words rise out of their firsthand awareness of this reality and in the process draw on and submit to the shared interpretive understandings in Christian tradition.

Such people one way or another will relate their own gifted awareness of reality coinherent in God to this very nature of God. Being made in the image of God is felt to be very real: we mirror God's nature, and yet God's nature is infinitely beyond. In this mirror we find that we are not ultimately separate from the rest of God's creation or from God (a dualistic theological view), nor are we completely one (monism); we are coinherent, a diversity in unity (pantheism).

Such contemplative awareness thus points to the givenness of community. Community is intrinsic to creation and to God. It does not have to be created or engineered. Indeed, it cannot be. It can only be realized, celebrated, and reverberated in different constellations of relationship.

Then what is the problem? Why is communing so difficult? Ultimately no one can tell us. There is a mystery to the existence of all those things that block community and leave behind so much suffering: the mystery of evil, sin, ignorance, freedom, and the general way God has somehow permitted life to be, from natural catastrophes to living by the sweat of our brow. Included in that permission, though, is the divine invitation to move inside of God's will toward the communing we yearn for: the ultimate community that scripture calls the kingdom of heaven, God's *shalom,* the messianic banquet, the new Jerusalem, where in the end God becomes all in all.

The way is pointed out and empowered through Jesus Christ, in whom is revealed the community we are called to be. This community has no intrinsic "outsides": "I am in my Father, and you in me, and I in you" (John 14:20); "I am the Vine, you are the branches" (John 15:5). The divine and human are coinherent in Christ, and by grace in us.

But even with the best intentions such community still experiences brokenness. Enter ego self-image! I spoke of this difficult interior friend in the last chapter. Let me continue its description here as background for viewing community, since it is so crucial to a contemplative understanding.

The reflective nature of self-image helps us to practically function in life personally and communally. But that same reflective nature tends to create a sense of identity that is self-contained. The resulting sense of hard separateness leaves us with a dilemma that we bring into community. On the one hand we feel the need to protect and assert this self-image, a need that reflects a hard sense of dualism: "I" am completely contained in this self-image, therefore "I" will treat the rest of reality according to the way it enhances or threatens this sense of self. Out of the widespread dominance of this orientation comes the necessity of moral laws for a community's functioning.

On the other hand, something in us is not satisfied with this view of self. We sense a larger belonging, a quality of incompleteness. A passion rises in us for pouring into the larger world and having the larger world pour into us. We want to reciprocate our bodies, emotions, creative images, and skills back and forth.

This desire for reciprocation reflects our true nature's coinherence. It drives us beyond our ego self-image's tendency to center reality on itself. Yet the tug in this direction is strong. At its height, a willfulness takes over and the pouring becomes destructive: we manipulate the world exclusively for our pleasure, protection, and power.

Even when self-image identity is hemmed in by some larger sense of self and community it can remain subtly dominating. We may spend a lot of time identifying with and serving others in a way that is still very attached to this self-image's enhancement and protection. Self-image now may include a communal identity as part of itself. This certainly is a step in the right direction. It may include a sense of God as well, but God still is primarily a cosmic bellhop or demanding parent, an outsider with whom our reflective self-image bargains for living room and approval. There is not yet the freedom to realize our full coinherence and our deepest identity in God.

This identity is not just in an image of God that enhances our self-image, but it is the deepest reality of self, the heart of self. It is not found in self-image, but in the spaciousness of God, who endows us with this reflective self-image as an aid for being in the world, for living on this plane of reality. When this realization dawns, we begin to pass from the old Adam to the new (1 Cor. 15:45). Community then takes on a fresh sense of possibility.

By looking at a few levels of community now, we can see just what differences this contemplative awareness can make.

COMMUNITY WITHIN THE BODY

The first level of community is the one within. Our bodies form one level of coinherence. On the physical plane this involves a vast array of interdependent cells in various dynamic configurations. But these physical properties are not hard substances. Under a microscope they are seen to be mostly space. What to the naked eye looks like a separate, frozen-in-place substance, under the microscope appears more like that contemplative vision of reality I earlier described: a dynamic, vibrant, transparent weave of forms, seemingly growing out of space—a kind of shaping of the space, ultimately created and sustained in being by some miraculous, pervasive power.

EXERCISE 10: EXPLORING COMMUNITY WITHIN

Close your eyes and let your imagination take you through your body with a focus on its spacious and miraculous quality. Emphasizing the spaciousness can include a sense of the openness of forms. Even the boundaries can be sensed more as shadings than as hard lines. Everything is growing out of a mysterious depth together, coinhering, belonging together, with forms dying and rising within this united process.[2]

After doing this for about fifteen minutes or longer, let your sense of body expand into a sense of presence within the great, cosmic Body of Christ. You need not try for any particular images of this Body; it is sufficient just to open your awareness in trust to the intimate vastness of all form that comes from God and is suffused with the Spirit of Christ. Be spaciously present there for about ten minutes or longer. End with a brief prayer of gratitude for the wonder of this interwoven community within and beyond.

Besides putting you in touch with the wondrous mystery of embodied community, such an exercise can help you to condition your sense of coinherence at other levels of community. It also challenges the tendency of ego self-image to create a hard, frozen, isolated sense of self. As that sense of self loosens, you begin to notice the great vibrant wealth of form and creativity that lies within us, and ultimately a sense of the Spirit as indweller. Yet you realize that this richness finally is not a private possession. It is more free and boundless than that, even though it is patterned through us, for our stewardship and appreciation.

You can be led to other levels of community then not only with a sense of coinherence but with an awareness of gifts to share. Thus you can move toward others without a sense of personal impoverishment with its consequent grasping need to be filled by them. You can approach others with the humble dignity of trusting that there is much within you that is of God, with the colorings of your own unique being. At the same time, knowing your coinherence, you can meet with others knowing your need for their giftedness to reverberate with yours, so that a fresh expression of life can be brought forward: a new expression of its love, creativity, and joy in God.

RELATING TO ANOTHER

Such fresh expression and life is seen most literally in the birth of a child that rises out of the love, joy, and creative capacity of its parents. The newborn infant is a paradigm for all levels of birthing, just as the sexual act from which it came is a paradigm for all levels of joining.

Let's stay with this sexual act for a minute. It is the oldest, most driven form of being with another. Behind it lies the amazing capacity with which we are born to attract and be attracted phyically. It draws people together who otherwise might never come together. It cuts through all kinds of differences. It is one of God's drives in us to commune and thus reflect the nature and goal of creation.

No enduring relationship with another person is without this magnetic drive in some form. It does not have to involve genital action or even sexual attraction. The appeal may be in the form of a person's voice, eyes, movement, or any of a myriad of other features that make their physical presence something we want to be near. Such attraction is inherent to our embodied existence, an existence hallowed in the Incarnation.

However, the Incarnation also leads us to orient that energy toward its divine Source and away from lostness and scatteredness in the world, whereby we are blindly driven by every impulse that comes along. Thus we have a long religious heritage of trying to "recollect" this great magnetic energy in us, in order to keep it connected with its life-giving Wellspring. In its lost and scattered form this energy can show itself as a negative attraction, such as hatred or resentment, or as a possessive positive attraction, such as envy or jealousy.

Thus "what to do" with this energy becomes an even larger issue of relationship. This question is not easily answered or carried out. We might simply try to bury the energy, leaving ourselves like stuffed closets whose doors tremble from the pressure of enclosure, in time leading to a kind of dried-up, embittered harshness. Or we might instead notice that this energy is capable of being turned in a different direction. We can open its narrow drivenness to a more generalized energetic presence that remains rooted in God, with a quality of open compassion. Exercises 11 and 12 can help us do this.[3]

EXERCISE 11: OPENING THE EMOTIONS TO GOD I

1. When your consciousness becomes dominated by a scattered magnetic energy that is quickly attached (positively or negatively) to the thought or presence of another person, remember that you have a choice. (a) You can just go with the emotion; (b) You can try to ignore or bury it; (c) You can try to analyze the emotion—its relational cause, meaning, moral and spiritual value, etc.; (d) You can simplify it, allowing its energy to become more available to God.

2. Here is a way to simplify it. (a) Note a current or recent strong emotion that has hooked your self-image; you have an image of yourself being attracted or repelled by someone. "I" am angry at "him" because of what "he" did to "me." (b) Instead of such elaboration of a subject-object level of involvement, you can go "backward" with the

energy. Instead of elaborating "I," "him," "because," you can dissolve these one by one: the "because," the "him," and finally the "I." Then what is left? Simply that raw wave of energy itself. It no longer has a driven subject and direction. The energy is available to be turned in any direction, especially to an open compassion that is not driven by ego self-image, but instead is available to God. At this point your sense of identity has shifted from the ultimacy of little self-image to the ultimacy of your big, spacious being in God. A sense of option, of emotional roominess, appears with this shift. Self-image finds its proper place as an aid to your presence with others rather than being an imperial definer of that presence. The expression of anger, love, and so forth, may still be appropriate in a situation, but it is more free from ego self-image identification and driveness.

REFLECTION QUESTIONS

1. Were you able to experience some transformation of the emotion's driven, directed energy into an open compassion, available for God?
2. What might make this transformation difficult for you?

EXERCISE 12: OPENING THE EMOTIONS TO GOD II

The intent of this exercise, as with the last, is to help you notice the attachment of particular emotions to ego self-image identification, and the possibility of turning to your deeper identity in God through the energy of these emotions. The last part of this exercise takes the intent one step further, however: into your capacity to be openly present with others and God beyond any emotion.

This exercise should come fairly late in the sequence of exercises, given its rather intense nature and need for understanding of self-image. Steps 6 and 7 can be carried out either alone or in pairs.

1. Sit a few feet from a wall and select any particular spot on it for your focus (Alternatively, all the following steps can be done with the eyes closed, with no external focus. Simply let the emotions rise without any particular object.)
2. Close your eyes. Be in touch with your intent to be present to God through and beyond your emotions.
3. Open your eyes and again let your gaze settle on that spot on the wall. (a) Look at this spot, and let yourself feel *fear*. Do this for three or four minutes. Try to sense that you are strongly identified with your ego self-image, which feels threatened and in need of protection. It is as if you are looking at a powerful person or object that you want to push away, to keep at a distance. Let

your facial muscles show this fear as a way of helping you get into it. (b) Now see if you can release yourself to God behind the fear. Note then how your over-identification with your ego self-image recedes and your self identified in God emerges with a confident, open quality. That wave of energy formed into fear may continue, but your identification with it is loosened. You feel a certain sufficiency in God at the center of your consciousness. (c) After three or four minutes has passed, close your eyes and relax a moment.

4. Open your eyes again onto the spot. (a) This time look with *desire:* a sense of attraction is taken over by your ego self-image in a way that you become strongly identified with the desire as a need to possess. You will feel a sense of personal impoverishment, an emptiness that demands to be filled, with an edge of greed or lust. There is an insistent quality of wanting to draw the spot toward you. (b) See if you can release yourself to God behind the desire, and notice that the results are similar to what happened in step 3. (c) Close your eyes and rest a moment.

5. Open your eyes again onto the spot. (a) Now look at it with *anger,* a sense of violation that is taken over by your ego self-image in a way that you become identified with it as a strong need to protect and lash out. You feel attached to this sense of violated ego self-image as your ultimate identity. As the threat increases, you may want to destroy the offender. Screw up your facial muscles in anger. (b) See if you can release yourself to God behind the anger. Notice that the results are similar to those in steps 3 and 4. In this case your identity that was hooked into the closed, dominating feeling of anger is loosened; your larger identity in God lets the anger's strong, confident, penetrating energy become available for whatever is called for. (c) Close your eyes and rest again.

6. This step can be done either looking at the spot on the wall or else sitting face to face with someone. (a) Look with *compassion*— an open energy, felt for a person's or object's well-being. If you are sitting with someone, you might want to focus on the bridge of the person's nose, both as a way of keeping your eyes still and of lightening self-consciousness. Let there be a deep, mutual identity in God, freeing an open presence that has no need to push away or pull toward you. Your ego self-image is available to the Spirit, as an aid for appreciative and compassionate presence. (b) Close your eyes and retain this quality of compassion. Note its similarity to your quality of consciousness in deep intercessory prayer, wherein you are opening life to God's compassion through you. (c) Relax a moment with your eyes closed.

7. Open your eyes again and look with the same compassion you just experienced, this time retaining it for at least five or ten minutes. During this time: (a) Let go in trust even your observer and its

self-image which helped you in the last step to be appreciative and otherwise consciously relational. Let everything melt into a self-forgetful, undivided, energetic presence. Trust that there is a quality of "knowing" inherent in this moment so that you do not need your collecting observer to catch and possess it.[4] Just allow a still, shared mind, deeply grounded in God. Leave nothing standing between you and the being of God and your neighbor, not even an image of these, realizing a naked, coinherent presence. (b) Close your eyes. Let a very simple prayer shape itself in you.

8. Allow at least ten minutes for silent journal keeping or relaxing after this intensive exercise.

REFLECTION QUESTIONS

1. Could you notice a shift in your identity, from attachment to self-image to identity in God, and its impact on your feelings of fear, desire and anger? (*Note:* Often people assume that they have been asked to disolve each emotion, but the instruction was not to release the *feeling* to God, but rather, to release your *self,* your *identity,* to God. The emotion might still remain in some form, but hopefully it no longer is attached to your ultimate sense of identity. Rather, it becomes a more readily available energy for God, not a narrow power that can take you over and cause you or someone else harm.)

2. Did you experience an open quality of compassion (in step 6) and notice the way your ego self-image was present as icon rather than idol (i.e., as helpful mediator of compassionate presence, rather than as a self-referencing barrier)?

3. Could you notice a certain playfulness, an appropriate flexibility of your feelings once you opened your identity to God, rather than feeling yourself as a passive pawn of them?

4. Do you sense that once you have released yourself to God behind the feelings, you would have a better capacity to discern and follow what really was called for in a given situation?

5. What happened to your awareness during the time you were able to be present between "observers" in step 7?

Exercise 11 and 12 are obviously very challenging when we let ourselves fully participate in them. Each of these exercises bears repeating to enable fuller integration of their teachings about ourselves, our emotions, our neighbor, and God. Such forms of attention to God through our strong emotions normally are left out of spiritual development. Usually feelings will be dealt with in terms of an understanding of emotional needs, moral impact, and forgiveness. Contemplative awareness contributes a further dimension: experiential awareness of an identity in God that is greater than our identity with ego self-image, with all the positive consequences for feelings and relationships discussed in this section.

FAMILY AND SPOUSE

Spouses, children, and other family members provide a special setting for spiritual community.[5] I don't know any kind of ongoing relationships that are more challenging spiritually. One reason for this is that our ego self-images usually are so bound up in these relationships that it is difficult to live out of our fuller identity in God. Here we are father, mother, wife, husband, son, daughter (and so forth—in an extended family). These identities take on great force (remember Jesus' difficulties when he went home to Nazareth!). Our identity with ourselves and one another at this level produces a role observer in us that judges and responds in terms of conditioned understandings of what it is to be a mother, son, and so forth.

However, if there is some sense of trust and security in the family, it is the most likely place that we will relinquish our observers at times and just be playfully or lazily present. Our locus of attention and attachment often is found at the level of sensual gratification during these times: indulging our appetites for all kinds of ordinary pleasures, from snacks to television to playing with the dog. Not only does our identity with ego self-image subside during these periods, but often our deeper identity in God as well. In their place is a kind of regressed, dulled sense of self that just reacts to the environment as it comes along.

Grace is a marvelously pervasive affair and God has ways of getting through to us in both of these states; indeed, both of them reflect a form of familial grace, yet a larger dimension of identity in God does not easily come through. Thus we need a third quality of presence in families, one that frees a larger sense of identity in God. This can be cultivated through a variety of collective spiritual practices that plant the seeds of this identity over the years, a few of which I have elaborated on in another book.[6]

I would like now to emphasize the presence that arises from individual rather than collective means. Behind this lies my experience with the great spiritual differences that normally are found among individuals in a family. Its members may or may not be able to valuably share certain practices together at a given time. Even if they do, these practices probably mean quite different things to different members. These differences are most obvious with children, but they are also true with spouses. They can become particularly noticeable when children have left home and spouses have more time together. Our different personalities and conditionings, and the different ways through which the Spirit shapes us, can lead to a very different "feel" for God between spouses. There may be periods when there is a strong overlap, but these periods can come and go as one person or the other changes.

If one spouse begins to sense a strong tug of the Spirit toward opening a larger identity in God, he or she often faces a temptation to feel "this is so lifegiving, I want my spouse to share it with me." That is a very natural desire, but unless there is some sense of call in the spouse, to pursue it can only lead to frustration. This is doubly true if the Spirit's invitation to one person includes an embracing of a more contemplative awareness, since this carries with it a sense of reality and personhood that challenges cultural as well as personal conditioning.

Sometimes God carries couples along the same path and at the same pace, but often this is not true, and perhaps this is no accident. There is no greater testing ground for what is evolving in us of God, than close family members who do not share the same spiritual hunger or responsiveness. If we become attached to what is happening on an ego self-image level, for example, if we feel possessive of a spiritual truth in a way that seems rigid, or that stimulates a sense of too much self-importance, or of having the one right way to God, then just being around the differences of our spouse or other family members is likely to challenge us!

One great need in families is to trust and respect the different ways that God is secretly at work in each person, and to support whatever has a quality of loving truth to it, however little we may understand. This does not mean that we cannot be challenging to one another, especially when loving truth seems missing, and inviting to each other when there is an openness, but where the different paths feel at least potentially legitimate, even if God is only tacitly present in one of them, we need to sense the positive side of this difference. We are left with more growing and correcting room and with an awareness of the great variety of ways to deeper realization of God. God can use our differences as channels of grace. I would say the same thing is true between members of religious communities and churches, as well as between close friends.

GOD MADE THEM MALE AND FEMALE

For men and women, in general, God can use differences as channels of grace. This mysterious complementarity of our human nature needs special attention.

We live in what is probably the most revolutionary historical period in terms of openness about what it is to be a man and a woman. This has brought confusion, dangers, and reaction in its wake, but it has also brought a new freedom that has implications for our spiritual development. I particularly mean the freedom for each of us to accept and slowly integrate, let "commune" together, what Carl Jung called our anima and animus, the stereotypically feminine and masculine dimensions of our being. Such an integration is not the same thing as spiritual maturity, but, as Gerald May has said, it can assist our psychological *capacity* for a fuller relationship with God.

The relationship of masculine and feminine, both within and between us, is a vast subject covered by a rapidly increasing amount of literature. However, there seems to be relatively little direct addressing of a central question of the spiritual life: "What does my experience (wounds, gifts, and perceptions) as a man or woman do to my prayer and sense of God?"

I will restrict myself to a few probings of this two-pronged question concerning the relationship of masculine and feminine within and between us, with a final word about one contemplative contribution. It is a question with which I and others at Shalem have struggled for many years. The insights of many people will be found mingled with my own, most especially those of my colleagues Gerald May and Dolores Leckey. I invite you, alone, or in mixed or single-sex groups, to answer the question for yourself. We all have our personal and often unexamined experience to elicit here.

The experience we bring to God has physical, genetic, psychological, and cultural conditionings. Let me mention just a few examples among a great many possibilities that might affect our relationship to God.

In my experience, men have felt great need or expectation for strong, competent performance, from sexual intercourse to the sports field to the job. Sometimes this takes the extreme form of very aggressive, controlling, competitive behavior. When this self-image identity and experience is brought to prayer, especially if one's image of God is masculine, one effect might be a sense of high expectation by God for performance. I recall a middle-aged minister once speaking of the enormous relief in his prayer when he finally experienced God just as an end-in-itself loving relationship, after decades of being dominated by a sense of demand for performance.

With the revolutionary new demands placed on women in Western society today, often, on top of the old demands, we may well see a similar effect in their relation to God. However, many women have told me that on the whole they feel a fuller drive toward relationships for the sake of relating with people, which may free their relationship with God to more easily be one of Lover than of demanding Judge.[7] Put negatively, if men most fear losing control with God (control being required for performance), women perhaps most fear being abandoned, if their priority is for the intimate relationship itself. But such speculative generalizations may well be blurred by the increasing pressures on women for high performance in every area of life (including

as lovers, which may make it more problematic relating to God as unconditional Lover).

Sensing God as Lover and as Mother seems to be made particularly
difficult by the relative lack of intimacy involved in an aggressive, controlling, outward moving, performance orientation. Such senses of God
also are rendered problematic for men to the extent they have great
difficulty in separating from their mothers. The struggle for independence from the potentially smothering power of the mother, and the
relative independence involved in performance, may bring a man to
prayer with a desire to avoid an intimate surrender to God as Lover
through either male or female imagery, but especially the latter. At the
same time, perhaps man's as well as woman's deepest yearning is for
just such surrender and vulnerability, which can be realized if there is
enough graced trust that this will lead to a liberated rather than oppressive life in God. The increasing nurturing role being accepted by
many men today may more easily allow this to occur for them.

I know a number of spiritually mature women who seem more free
to relate passionately to God through male imagery, sometimes with
erotic experiences that they may or may not find embarrassing. A male
image might be oppressive for women as well, but ironically enough,
perhaps no more so than for men, who often seem to have more trouble with intimacy through the image of either sex (though again the
more nurturing norms for men today may be changing this). Perhaps
this is one reason why I have noted fewer men than women participating in groups devoted to direct relationship with God, men more
often seeming to prefer a more personally distanced relationship found
in service, organizational leadership, and conceptual and legal order-
ing. These are vitally needed strengths and callings, but are not substitutes for a more direct relationship. Both men and women are called
to listen for the universal invitation to personal communion as well as
service.

The changing roles of men and women today may be bringing more
balance for both men and women in these different ways of relating
to God. Indeed, the emerging "post-liberation" man and woman may
end up with a certain amount of reversed experience to bring to God:
more performance orientation for the woman, more relational for the
man, and a lot of confusion in between. Perhaps, though, we can look
forward to a better acceptance and integration of so-called masculine
and feminine qualities in each of us. This would free us to bring more
flexibility to our prayer, and more availability to God for whatever may
be called for in the relationship. One way or another this will include
both intimacy and a courageous responsiveness to the divine invitations
we are given.

This integration seems more likely to happen in midlife or later,
when women and men begin to sense a special restlessness inside them.

It is important that the restlessness be seen as a call to "fill out" what is missing (intimate surrender, focused performance, and so forth), rather than as a call to new ways of reinforcing what is already dominating them. The former interpretation leads in trust toward greater fullness in God. The latter leads to reinforced attachment to the way one is, an attachment that can lead to sterility in one's relationship to God.

Gay, lesbian, and bi-sexual women and men face the same basic experiences and struggles in their prayer, but with the added dimension of an often more shaky or negative self-image that creates more fear, anger, and yearning. They come to prayer in part with the experience of an oppressed minority. Rather than being a negative factor, however, the very suffering of such people, as with any oppressed group, can become a graced means of surrender to God if they are willing and able to release any overattachment to this identity (positive or negative) at the ego self-image level.[8]

A CONTEMPLATIVE CONTRIBUTION

Release from overattachment to our sexual identities is a hope for all of us, which brings us to a special contemplative contribution to sexuality. God created us male and female. These dimensions are part of our giftedness. At the same time, in Christ there is neither male nor female (Gal. 3:28). We carry our experience of maleness and femaleness to God in our ego self-image, will all its passion, performance, distinctiveness, and complementarity. However, we are called to relativize this image, along with all others, to our larger identity in God. Contemplative awareness draws us affirmatively through many images and experiences to a more inclusive presence in the Mind/Heart of Christ, which includes but goes beyond our sexuality and beyond sexual images of God.

This is true in the relationship between a man and a woman as well. We need to respect our complementarity and interdependence as gifts of God, one more avenue through which we can glimpse the holy Ground of life. The image of God is expressed in the *relationship* of men and women, and the heart of this relationship is its mysterious, spacious, loving center in God. We need to approach such a relationship with the innocence of entering unknown ground. We come open to what we do not know fully, just as we come before God. The relationship then is free to draw out fruits beyond our imagining, the chief of which is a deepening realization of God's subtle, caring life among us.

Such an orientation to one another also helps to save us from substituting our personal relationships for our fuller relationship in God. As Gerald May has pointed out, we symbolically identify romantic love and spiritual experience. Our language reveals this identification. Both mystical and sexually erotic language include words like *rapture, joy, delight, divine, transport, yearning,* and *love.*

Romantic love often feels unconditional and sufficient, and yet it is not, as we see when it so easily shifts to hate, tedium, and possessiveness. It is a manifestation of spiritual energy, full of passion, but no person is capable of fully satisfying the hunger it manifests. To try to make another person (or group of people) a completely sufficient focus for our love is to create an idol that finally will crumble from the pressure. In disillusionment we may think that we just need to keep searching for the right person, or else we may give up altogether on the passion in us and settle for a bland, low-energy existence with God and one another.

But that loving passion in us is divine. We need this graced energy to melt the power of our fear, lethargy, and smaller identifications, so that our unconditional identity in God can open and reveal the one sufficient boundless center for our passion. There in divine agapie love we live in authentic union. The world is together; self-definition recedes. We know a different quality of experience than in erotic love. In erotic love the world disappears in disassociating mutual fusion and narrow self-definition remains strong. Such love can be a gifted expression of the boundless love of God from which it is derived, but it is relative to that larger love and needs to open to its fullness.

EXERCISE 13: MEN AND WOMEN: REALIZING OUR OPEN CENTER IN GOD

One way for a couple to help realize the shared, open center of their relationship in God is to practice the following exercise:

1. Sit closely, facing each other at eye level.
2. Close your eyes briefly and be in touch with your desire for God.
3. Open your eyes and look either at the bridge of the other's nose, or else look through the pupil of one of the other's eyes.
4. For at least fifteen minutes, gently lighten your self-consciousness. Let your mind be very open, energetic, and still. Let any thoughts, feelings, or observers that rise pass by without trying to grasp them. In this way drop toward your deeper unitive identity in God. Be present to God through one another, with a simple open awareness.
5. *(Optional)* If you want to try and deepen your mutuality still further, spend at least another fifteen minutes slowly sensing yourself becoming the other person, and the other becoming you: a

very simple, thought-less, willing, energetic exchange. Let the resulting intimacy open thought-lessly into God.

6. Close your eyes. Relax in silence a few minutes. Then share together your sense of a shared open center in God, and perhaps some sense of its implications for your relationship.

SOLITUDE AND COMMUNITY

How do we live together in such a way that we allow room for the evolution of subtle growth processes in our divine and human relationships?

Beyond the hints already given, I would like to hold up one dimension of intentional spiritual community that can be particularly crucial: the need for a rhythm of solitude and coming together. Contemplative tradition has placed great weight on the need for silence in a community's life. Behind this lies much spiritual wisdom. Above all, solitude helps to unveil, and keep unveiled, "the delusion that we can be saved through human interaction."[9]

This delusion is a powerful hope of many people in communities, from the small nuclear family through the larger religious community. Behind the delusion is a belief that if one can just join a community where everybody is trying to be open and loving with their feelings, thinking, working, praying, and playing, and where everybody is committed to trying to fix one another up in whatever way seems needed, God's Reign will come. We think we can will this into being if we are sincere and energetic enough. Such an expectation will founder on the hard realities of human limitation and difference. It is a form of works-righteousness that must fail, just as erotic love finally fails as a sufficient arena for our spiritual energy.

The good news, though, is that its very failure becomes a graced opportunity. In that failure, if we can avoid the temptation to turn cynical and narcissistic, we find ourselves turning to God's mercy. At first this may come out of a lingering attachment to salvation through human interaction: "God, help us to get it just right together." But as our turn to God deepens, we find that our ego self-image lightens its identity with the sufficiency of human interaction, both our own and others. We begin to notice a larger identity in God that appears in solitude, and with it a larger sense of community.

In many of the exercises that I have suggested in this book we can be helped to realize the inclusive nature of authentic solitude. Far from being a time of isolation and exclusion, our opening to God in solitude reveals the full coinherence of God's creation. We realize our inherent belonging beyond any human effort to construct a belonging.

Such an experience of community in solitude sends us back to human relationships with a new freedom. We no longer have to demand the community to fill some poverty of perfected relationship that we are feeling, for we return to the community with a richness of relationship in God. We no longer have to suffer the impossible demand from others in the community for our perfected relationship to fill their sense of neediness, for others have been opened in solitude to community in God as well (hopefully!).

We now are free for spiritual community to become what it really is capable of: a group of people rooted in that spacious divine center I spoke of in a man-woman relationship, and from that central identity feeling free to celebrate and draw out the sacred, distinctive, latent godliness found in each person and in each collective action. At the same time everyone is free from expecting too much from one another. Our real hope has shifted from mutual controlling, securing, and self-justifying expectations to a reliance on God's already rich, active presence in and among us, being manifest in ever-surprising ways.

Because of the difficulty of retaining this large identity in God, everyone will be in and out of it. Everyone can be expected to manifest the little ego identifications that are part of our broken human nature, as well as the larger physical and mental ills that are ours. These can be accepted and attended with the compassion that Jesus showed for our brokenness, including compassion on our own ego reactions of anger and fear. We can become channels of the Spirit for one another with energetic concern. This process becomes a learning ground for our concern and action in the larger human and ecological community we share in God.

All the brokenness presses us back to solitude again and again, wherein our larger identity and community in God emerges with fresh strength and sanity. Again and again we move back into physical community as more recollected beings of God's peace.

This was Jesus' rhythm: withdrawal and community. But the withdrawal then and now is never from community, only to community in a different form, and for community. This rhythm teaches us how to be in the world but not of it, in and for community, but of God. It does not guarantee such a result, certainly not steadily. It is a structure though, that cultivates our availability to Christ's Spirit, through which we become ever more fully who we are called to be. Through Christ the whole body grows, and with the proper functioning of the members joined firmly together by each supporting ligament, the body is built up in love (paraphrase of Eph. 4:16).

Each community setting must develop the appropriate rhythm of solitude and community for itself. A family or larger community might agree upon daily and weekly sabbath time together.[10] This may be communal time, or it may be largely tailored to individuals' schedules if the community is not of an ordered monastic style. Silence can always be part of collective worship, even if it is only pregnant pauses with grace at meals for a family, or between lessons and other actions in a liturgy.[11] In busy families sabbath time might begin to happen on slow and quiet walks together. Longer periods in solitude for individuals are more likely to be assured if they are taken at the same time and in the same place each day.

STABILITY

Spiritual community on every level includes the task of encouraging one another to hear the deep invitation to "follow me": to follow Christ into *Abba's* heart. There we will be given a larger identity, and that identity can provide a radiance for the community in whatever big or little ways may be called for. Something in us, a smaller and divisive identity, resists the unifying power of this larger identity. We need all the supportive and challenging help from one another that we can get as we go through the lifetime struggle to let our larger identity prevail.

As we have seen, this help can be provided by protecting time for one another's solitude, and by a generally accepting and encouraging presence. We cannot make things happen for one another. We can just keep turning our eyes toward the community's true Center and be alert for God's timing.

Since this is a permanent task, we can provide one another with a sense of long-haul commitment. This is one of the spiritual functions of vows at every level of community (beginning with the vows of baptism). We are saying, "Yes, I know this is a long-term, mysterious, easily side-tracked, yet promising journey. I feel called to be with this person (perhaps a spiritual friend or spouse) on pilgrimage, and with this (family, church, or religious) community, and I pledge myself to stay with them through hard times and easy."

Such shared commitment provides a stable communal environment that we can relax into for the long haul, rather than a community of convenience wherein we and others are forever on trial, looking for a quick fix, and moving on if it doesn't happen. Longterm vows express our humility: we know we need support, challenge, and fellowship. Such vows also express the calling of God in us: responsible community life is part of our inheritance in Christ.

Despite our need, such vows are not easily made. Marriage vows are taken, but I think rarely with this shared spiritual heart. A spiritual friend is found, but we have a way of psychologizing a lot together and evading God. Churches are joined, but often for a host of reasons that do not center on our deepest calling. Even with an intention of such centering, communities can be crippled by their failure to open to God the three intrinsic areas of community life symbolized by the monastic vows of poverty (our possessions), chastity (our passions), and obedience (our authority). These are easily taken over by our little self's confused or willful drive to control life apart from God.

Thus our potential spiritual communities are ambiguous. Sometimes they become so evasive of God, and so destructive of love, that we are called to leave them. We hope, though, that with all their failings, such covenanted communities can become channels of grace for one another and for the world (even in their failures sometimes!). For that we must steadily pray, remembering that intercession is communal prayer, communing with God for the community we share, praying for the fruits of the Spirit that mark real community (Gal. 5:22ff.).

CHAPTER 6

Re-membering

"Re-membering" life in God, letting what has been cut off and scattered be found and transfigured together, is at the heart of spiritual formation. I have sought to convey means for cooperating with this graced process through the body, sound, sight, and community. Now I will focus on *memory*, which affects all the other dimensions through the imprints of experience it carries into the present.

Over the years these imprints often become attached to our self-image, reinforcing their effect on us. Instead of being helpful experience of the past that we bring to the moment's understanding, appreciation, and discernment, "hallowed" memories, they take over the newness of the moment and turn it into a reflection of the old, thus becoming "haunting" memories.

Our brains have physiologically contributed to this tendency by becoming habituated to the ongoing power of these memories. Our brains cause them to appear even when we do not will it: in our dreams and in our waking hours. Thus our brains in effect become addicted to them. Insofar as these are attached to our self-image, they become identified with who we are. Whether they are painful or pleasurable, we become familiar with them as part of who we are. Our wills then often cooperate with memories in reinforcing their power as we prefer to retain the familiar and predictable to anything new.

When we sink into our unpossessive larger identity in God, though, we participate in making all things new (Rev. 21:5). Every moment is a fresh moment of the Spirit, unless we chain it to the staleness of a past moment. When we identify with our ego self-image as our ultimate self, we will likely fear this freshness in our clinging to the familiar, as much as we might yearn for it in our dim sense of its calling.

The result is an attempt to eat our cake and have it too. We find a way to retain the ultimacy of the familiar and yet to create an illusion of freshness. In its most obvious form this can be seen when we find a new kind of makeup, a new house, a new place for vacation, or a new job; yet we carefully maintain the same "memorized" self-attachment. A new exterior is accumulated, and new experience, but these are carefully plastered on top, chained to the old.

How can we open this chain of memories to God? How can we become more present in the fullness and freshness of this moment that has never been? These are questions about conversion of memory. A contemplative contribution to this involves an understanding of the relation between the linear time that ego self-image considers real and functional, and God's great Time, God's Eternity, in which everything is present at the same time.

Our self-image identity, which is tied up in linear time, feels dependent on an accumulation of the little things that occur along the way. If these memories were to disappear, we fear that nothing of "us" would be left, so we cling to the past rather than open it to God's "now." Self-image identity is basically very conservative in this way.

At the same time, we sense the poverty of this accumulation. We want to keep it all, we fear to let it go, yet it is never enough. In response we might bloat what we already have in order to fill this sense of incompleteness. We might try to enhance our family memory in some way, perhaps spending an inordinate amount of time tracing, embellishing, and identifying with our family tree. Or we might do the equivalent related to some particular social, political, physical, or educational dimension of our experience, giving a great amount of time to the glorification of a particular school, nation, sport, or other part of our experience. Authentic practical or playful attention to such causes are replaced by an idolatrous over-identification.

Another response to the sense of poverty might be an attempt to reject the impoverished past time and strike out for a different future time, some revolutionary new set of experiences: a new self and/or community or society. There is a boldness in this effort that goes beyond the attempt to simply have a new exterior while clinging to the past. Unfortunately, though, this bold attempt eventually founders on the impoverished sense of time that is still a determining conditioner. No matter how beautiful the dream of the new, it will never finally fulfill human beings if it is exchanging one impoverished view of time and self for what turns out to be another. This does not mean that such a vision may not be called for. We are called to provide the best "linear time" circumstances that we can, but this "bestness" needs to include a fuller sense of time.

We live in *two* dimensions of time, equivalent to the two dimensions of our identity. Linear time is a functional time related to the functional quality of our ego self-image identity. Like that identity, though, it is relative to our larger identity in God. What happens to time when we are most fully in that larger identity awareness? It loses its linear boundaries. What we would call past, present, and future when our functional ego self-image is operative now no longer describes our reality.

Time instead becomes the dynamic quality of an inclusively present reality. We become privileged as children of God to share in the reality behind such classical statements about God in relation to time as: "God is equidistant from past, present, and future." "God's center is everywhere and circumference nowhere." We cannot make such statements about our possessive ego participation in reality. That would be psychotic megalomania. But when we relinquish our functioning at this ego level we can participate to varying degrees in that larger awareness that cannot be possessed. In that awareness, formed reality pulses, it is "timed out" in an ever-present way. Contemporary physicists in their own way have noted this mysterious quality of "great time," along with contemplatives of all deep religious traditions.[1]

Let me emphasize that this quality of time need not invalidate or diminish the reality and value of linear time. You will recall my mention of our experience in solitude giving us a richness that we bring back to community living in linear time. We bring an awareness that can free us to be in community without making false demands upon it, and with an easier availability of our own gifts for it. I am referring to the height of that same awareness here.

When we bring its sense of great, open time into the linear time of our functional ego level of living, we bring a certain richness that frees linear time to be what it can be and not what it cannot. Since our own identity is less ultimately tied up in linear time then (knowing we are in the world but not of it), we bring to it less desperation, less drivenness, less fear, and more discerning energy and authentic concern. We bring more freedom for our own compassion and creativity to live in called-for ways.

There are some special exercises that can help alleviate our tendency toward strong self-image attachments to accumulated memories that block or distort our openness to God in the living present. Historically these exercises would come under such broad headings as *repentance, confession, healing,* and *reconciliation.* These words have a rich history of meanings and practices. I want to restrict myself here, though, to addressing ways that relate our self-image identities and our larger identity in God.

Repentance involves an invitation and timing of God's grace drawing out our willingness to release our ego self-image attachments and the behaviors that result from them. The consequence is *metanoia,* meaning "conversion"—converting the dominating level of our identity from a protective, aggrandizing sense of contained self, to our larger self in God.

This is not a once in a lifetime moment, though we may experience one or more particularly powerful times that dramatically shift our orientation. Full conversion, in which our wills, feelings, thoughts, bodies, imaginations, and memories all find themselves melded into the mind of Christ regularly, is a lifetime process (indeed, to faith, a process that continues beyond this lifetime).

In Christ, though, we find a fresh empowerment of this conversion process, a new initiative of God's mercy available for us. In trust we can turn to this mercy, which outlasts our sinfulness. Our sinfulness is our willful turning away from God, out of a desire to enhance an ego-centered sense of reality, or out of our fear of losing that sense.

EXERCISE 14: OPENING OUR SELF-IMAGES TO GOD

A fundamental level of confession involves releasing our accumulated little self-images that in turn influence so many of our actions and attitudes. These images are particular colorings of our ego self-image. The basic intent of this form of confession is to release their tendencies to become ultimate self-definitions, usurping our full, gifted name hidden in God. "I have called you by name, you are mine" (Isa. 43:1). In baptism we are given a particular name, and the name of Christ, through which we are called to open into our mysterious fullness that is known in God alone.

Trusting our ultimate full name in God helps to free us from becoming enslaved and limited by any names given us by others, or by ourselves. Such freedom in turn weakens our tendency to *ultimately* protect, justify, and identify with these self-images. Then the self-images become free to find their sane place in our functional daily living as transparencies, icons of our larger identity and purpose in God.

Thus this confession involves exposing our clinging self-images, that they may be opened to God where they are insulated, loosened where they are tightly binding, released where they are compelled or false, relativized where they are absolutized, and made transparent to the mercy of God. Mercy is God's free love of us beyond our works, God's sustaining of us as literal offspring who are unconditionally valued. Our confession is made from the stance of our great dignity in that love, an intrinsic dignity far deeper than any merited love could bestow. Thus we make confession, in whatever form, as a means of affirming our identity in this deepest source, and of releasing whatever would take its place and thereby diminish us and others.

This exercise is structured for two persons, sitting at eye level, close together but without touching. Decide between you who will be going first (this will apply later in the exercise). If this pairing is done within a group, individuals may want to be free to choose their own partners.

1. Close your eyes. Let yourself be in touch with any anxiety you have now; pray for your opening in trust to God. Now be in touch

with your yearning to release the overbearing power of whatever images take the place of your true being in God. Take a slow, deep breath and seek to relax into your underlying trust and hope.

2. Open your eyes and focus loosely on the bridge of the other's nose in order to lighten your self-consciousness and keep your eyes steady. Let yourself look through the surface of the person, seeking their heart in God, caring and praying for them at this deepest level.

3. Now seek to let your *self* be seen by God through the other person; let them be an icon of God for you.

4. For at least the next five minutes (timed by the leader, if this is being done in a group), the person who has volunteered to go first begins the process by asking the question: "Who are you?" After the other person has given a self-image, the first person responds with: "The Lord (or God) is merciful," then immediately repeats the question, "Who are you?", which is answered with a different image. This back and forth process continues for the minimal five minute period. The responder should use only simple, one word or phrase self-images, without commentary (e.g., father, daughter, teacher, lover, fearful). These might have negative, positive, or neutral connotations. That makes no difference, since all are capable of taking the place of God. They should be allowed to come as spontaneously as possible. If some of these images feel too hard to share, they can be withheld until a later time (see step 5).

5. If the exercise is done in a group, the leader rings a bell or claps at the end of this time, and everyone is asked to close their eyes. The person answering the questions continues in silence for several minutes with any images that he or she felt were too difficult to share out loud, listening after each one for the silent response from God, "I am merciful". Meanwhile, the other person sits in silent prayer for the partner.

6. The leader (if in a group) signals the beginning of the second round, during which time the two people exchange roles. Step number 5 is then repeated.

7. Now with eyes closed both persons seek to rest for three or four minutes in their deep identity in God, through and beyond any image.

8. End with a silent sense of appreciation, to the extent you are able, for God's mercy through another, and for your liberating identity in God.

9. The partners may feel moved to briefly hold each others' hands in silence and give one another a hug before moving into ten minutes of silent journal keeping and/or rest time.

REFLECTION QUESTIONS

In the pairs that met, reflect together on your experience, paying special attention to these questions.

1. What does God's mercy do to your self images?
2. What does resting in your deep imageless identity in God do to your sense of God and self?

Homework. For homework, a group or couple could practice saying (or writing), "The Lord (or God) is merciful" to self-images as they are noticed, seeking to rest in God briefly beneath them, where at its purest there is no image of self or God left standing, just a mutual real presence.

If this exercise is repeated later, you might want to extend the time, especially for the question and answer exchange. This might be extended to ten or fifteen-minute periods, giving people time to wear out the images and perhaps come to a spontaneous point of imageless presence, wherein they rest in their larger identity in God. As I hope is clear from all that has been said in this book, this identity is not disassociated from the present moment, but rather opens the moment to its fullness in God. As we shall discuss later, this quality of presence is the ground for truly discerning action in the world.

EXERCISE 15: DAILY EXAMEN

This practice is a special kind of examen. *Examen* normally refers to a brief daily (or other block of time) period where you examine the day's thoughts, feelings, and actions in terms of how God seemed to be present and how you responded. This is a way of going through your memory of the day, drawing its grace to your awareness. The following examen gives weight to contemplative awareness.

1. Relax your mind for a minute. In your intent drop to your larger identity in God, desiring to be in touch with God's presence in the day.
2. Don't try hard to find something. Just be very still and open, listening for what might rise from the day. As it does, notice any sense of its graced character with gratitude. Then notice the way you were present in that time. If you remember a strong, protective holding on to ego self-image, you might pray "Lord (or God) have mercy," very simply desiring the attachment to that image to lighten (as in exercise 14). If on the contrary you notice that ego self-image was only lightly present, functioning as a vehicle of understanding and activity without a character of ultimacy, you can simply smile to God with thanksgiving. Thus you are noticing both the hidden presence of God in the day, and your own way of participating in, missing, or resisting that presence.

This examen need not be long, heavy, or analytical. Rather it can be a light, open glance at the day for about five or ten minutes, with a desire for its fragments to be recollected in God.

HEALING

Jesus spent a lot of time drawing together what was separated from the reality of God's nature in and among us. God was in Christ reconciling us, who were lost through the power of sin (paraphrase of 2 Cor. 5:18–19). The power of sin includes our sometimes willful, sometimes helpless attachments to images of self that separate us from our true nature in God.

In the ego empire-building and protecting that comes from that separating identity, we create further separations of mind, body, feelings, and will. With others we reverberate that brokenness. Fragmentation, personally and socially, proceeds apace. Our memories and bodies are pocked with the results: many hurts and injustices given and received; many residues of fear, resentment, defense, and sickness. In the midst of all this, we desperately need healing. Healing begins with a trust that wholeness exists and that it is available for us in our turning to God.

Contemplative awareness reveals the wholeness that is present at the heart of reality. In our larger identity in God, we realize that coinherence; we taste its reconciling energy. It is out of that awareness in God raised to its fullness that Jesus radiated God's healing power. Again and again he called on people's faith in God's reconciling presence at every level of our being. The mind of faith is the mind that willingly opens to that personal presence. It cannot know this presence directly with reflective self-image, but the presence can be energetically trusted.

We cannot, however, assume that we will receive what our ego self-image might understand as healing. Our egos are very caught up in symptoms of brokenness. God in Christ promises to be about a deeper work of healing in the fundamental *sources* of brokenness. "I came that they may have life, and have it abundantly" (John 10:10). That life rises from an identity that ultimately flows from the wholeness of God rather than from any self-contained source. This identity with God is the fundamental healing. Physical, mental, and social symptoms of brokenness may be healed along the way to this Great Reconciliation, this central "conversion of memory," or they may follow from it. They may also continue to exist, as did St. Paul's "thorn in the flesh," concerning which the risen Christ told him: "My grace is sufficient for you, for my power is made perfect in weakness" (2 Cor. 12:9).

There are many mysterious ingredients in this process that include God's timing, our own and others' willingness, our inheritance of personal and social sin, our need for purging, the drawing of others to God through our suffering (and vice-versa), and the strange frailty and ignorance of our nature. We cannot be assured of the little healings that our little minds conceive. But we can image and ask for them in the power of our faith, hoping for the best, yet trusting that God's grace is not always the same as our view of healing. In the end all will be well. Along the way there is much enduring pain and much amazing healing mixed into this shadowed side of heaven.

In the meantime, we can open ourselves as vessels of and for God's healing the best way we can. In the process we need to remember the many levels of healing this might involve: broken individuals, the wounded social-political fabric, and our ruptured ecosystem.[2]

EXERCISE 16: CONVERSION OF MEMORY

This exercise provides one way of being an intentional vessel of healing for yourself, with an accent on conversion and healing of memory.

1. Sit quietly. For about five minutes seek to let your mind move into its deep identity in God, where everything is coinherent and open.

2. Ask God that you be shown something in your memory (which includes dreams) that has been cut off from God's radiant wholeness. This might be a particular destructive relationship, event, pattern of life, or more generally some particular racial or ethnic group, with your attendant feelings and actions. As it rises, notice your response. Ask yourself if this is a memory that you think ought to be reconciled but which you really aren't willing and ready to let be transformed yet, or rather one that you truly yearn be opened now to the healing power that we see in Jesus' ministry. Offer any resistance you feel to God. If it is strong, perhaps this prayer of offering is as far as you can go at this point with this particular memory. But you may feel a yielding of the resistance inside and a willingness to proceed.

3. If you feel a willingness to proceed, let your intent be to gently draw into the memory with energetic faith, God's opening, reconciling Spirit in Christ. With long, slow breaths, seek to breathe in that bright, radiant energy; let it pervade every aspect of that memory if you can, including any other people involved. Let your imagination participate in envisioning reconciliation. Let your intent include any needed forgiveness. Be honest about this, though, and try to recognize any residues of unwillingness to forgive at this time. On your long, slow outbreath, seek to release to God whatever separating power is in that memory: resentment, fear, willfulness, etc. Continue this practice for about ten minutes, or as long as seems called for.

4. You may or may not consciously notice some graced conversion of this memory, some transformation of its fragmented energy into the flowing energy of God's Spirit. You may notice some effect later more than now. You may even notice a different kind of healing than you were focused upon. The important thing is not to grasp hard for some preimagined result. Rather, try to return to your largest identity in God where you began, thankful for God's healing power in whatever form

it may be manifest. Seek to simply rest in the wholeness of that open awareness. Trust that this is the steady background foundation for the slow foreground gathering of whatever has fallen outside God's radiance.

God's Reign is already among us, but its full gatheredness slowly and mysteriously evolves through us as the time, including our willingness, is truly ripe. As a result, such a process of healing prayer may need to be repeated a number of times over months and years, as we seek to let the hard edges of a particular memory be worn away by God's radiance. All the time, though, we need to remain rooted in the wholeness that is always present at the Center.

EXERCISE 17: HEALING THROUGH OTHERS (FOR USE WITH ANOTHER PERSON OR GROUP)

In chapter 2, on embodiment, I pointed out that touch has been seen as a vehicle of the Spirit from the earliest days of the Church. The hands especially can be a wondrous vehicle of healing spiritual energy. They extend the Incarnation among us. We share with Christ in God's power for healing reconciliation. Just as with ourselves, though, we do not know for sure the kind of healing that may be called for at this time in another person.

You can ask the other person (or group) to go through steps 1 through 3 of the last exercise. Alternatively, you can simplify and broaden these to a single step: "Let rise from your heart what you sense most needs healing in you—physically, mentally, or spiritually—that you yearn for and feel ready to carry forward today." Toward the end of the third step, or after the alternative single step, lay your hands on the top or sides of the other's head (who may be in a sitting, kneeling, or lying position). In a group all can do this in pairs, or three or four people can lay hands on one person at a time (this has the advantage of reducing a sense of "me" as the healer). As you lay on hands, let your faith in God's healing power be as strong as possible, and yet very open for the form it might take. As the famous late spiritual healer Olga Whorrall told a friend of mine involved in a healing ministry, "Just let your mind go blank." That blankness is the openness of our mind for being a channel of God's reconciling will in whatever shape may be called for now.

Utter a brief prayer for healing, such as, "Merciful God, bring forward the healing of _____as you would have it, that he (or she) may be free to more fully glorify you in his (or her) life and work; in Jesus' Name we give you thanks."

If this exercise is being done for one another in pairs within a group, with hands laid on one another at the same time rather than separately, each person needs to go through the following two steps internally. First, for a minute let your minds and hands be open for God's healing of the other person. Then shift your attention to yourself: become aware of the other's hands on your head and be open to God for your healing. The group leader can offer a general healing prayer for everyone at the end, before people withdraw their hands.

A final step in groups then could be to have everyone gather in a circle with hands joined and let other people and world situations come to mind in the silence. Vicariously lay hands on them; try to imagine God's healing light filling them; pray for this to be true. The leader could end with a brief prayer of thanksgiving and praise. One of the values of this extra step is its capacity to reinforce a sense of the inclusiveness of the healing circle. Healing is not meant just for me or you, but for every dimension of God's creation. It is not a private affair; it spills us over into prayer and work for the world's reconciliation.

REFLECTION

In pairs or as a group, people can reflect upon their experience and wonderings about healing related to themselves and to the world. Particular attention might be paid to the sense of relation between the wholeness of their larger identity in God, and those often stubborn fragments of life that fall outside this wholeness that need healing.

DEATH AND CHANGE

"Re-membering" life may founder in the face of death, which looks like a dis-membering of life from life. Our memories are full of deaths: people, animals, places, stages of life, and ways of living and seeing. These often are painful memories. They continue to haunt us if our self-image will not let them go as necessary to our present existence, or at least let them be lightened. Separations of all kinds then may well become avoided at all costs. We live terrified by loss. We seek to secure and freeze present forms of life in every way we can. The reality of death is repressed at all costs.

However, if death has found its graced or at least neutral edge, we do not need to live so fearful of its many faces. God gives us the pattern for true life in the Paschal Mystery of Jesus, which is marked by trusting relinquishment of life to God and the rise of transformed life. Death is not a dismemberment of God's wholeness. It is a dimension of it. When we are overattached to our ego self-image, however, we inevitably dread whatever that image cannot retain for itself. That means a lot of dread, because we cannot finally retain anything for a separately contained self.

Life is a process, a movement of constantly reshaping forms. This very minute our bodies are changing. We can hold nothing still for long. The vibrancy of God's creation reconstellates life forms endlessly. And yet I think all that can be ultimately lost is the illusion of self-containment. When we let ourselves drop to our larger identity in God, there is nothing left to fear. We realize our true Home, that which endures. We are intimately connected with the One who shapes us into being with a privileged reflective ego capacity through which we share God's creative love. But in Christ "it is no longer I who live, but Christ who lives in me" (Gal. 2:20). Our locus of identity shifts from the ultimacy of ego self-image, to the deathless life of God through us.

Such an awareness and faith radically shifts our sense of death. Whatever of us that is of God will not die. Our particular future embodiment in the communion of saints we cannot know, but we can trust. The same is true in the ongoing little deaths of this life. We cannot know what form of life will emerge beyond, but we can trust beyond our fears. Our ego self-image thereby becomes more free to function as facilitator of God's buoyant present.

That facilitation includes a caring and defense of our own and others' lives. We have been willed into being by God; we carry the dignity of inspirited, "inspired" bodies. We fear and detest their wanton misuse and loss. Yet this is from the perspective of life in God and loses the destructive ultimacy of caring from the narrow perspective of self-contained ego. That perspective is often with us too. None of us escapes its exiling power. But something in us remembers its relativity to our larger life in God. With St. Paul we trust that "neither death nor life . . .will be able to separate us from the love of God in Christ Jesus our Lord" (Rom. 8:38–39, RSV).

EXERCISE 18: REFLECTION FROM THE EDGE OF DEATH

Ignatius Loyola recommended meditating upon our lives from the vantage point of our deathbeds as a way of helping us better discern what is called for in our lives now. This follows the prayer of Psalm 90:12. "So teach us to number our days, that we may get a heart of wisdom."

Standing in our imaginations on the edge of death can be a fine challenge to our tendency to repress death and desperately (though usually unconsciously) try to secure ourselves from it through much that we do. In a sense we are always standing on the edge of our physical death, which is but a breath away. As humans we rarely know the time and place it will, finally, be, but we know it will be, and that we live finally by grace. This need not be morbid. Repressing death is morbid. Facing God and life through death's reality is life giving: we are helped to live more vitally and truly now, knowing that our time is limited and precious in God's eyes.

This exercise is one way to let awareness of death be a spiritual discipline.

1. Sit or lie down quietly, imagining that you have been told you are about to die. Seek to notice the difference between your dominant self-image's fear of loss, and the confidence of your larger identity in God that rises as you relinquish the dominance of that self-image. Try to note the difference between a loss of continued ego self-image, and a trust in the abidingness of your identity in God.

2. Open your memory to God. You may choose to focus on recent months, or you may want to be open to anytime in your life. (a) What rises when you ask: "How have I been a blessing for others?" Give thanks as these moments pass by. Note how your larger identity in God touched into those times. Continue for ten to fifteen minutes or as long as seems called for (in step b, as well). (b) What rises when you ask: "In what particular ways and times have I clung to ego self-image as my ultimate self, and with what consequences for my life and others?" Especially note any times when there seemed present an invitation and freedom to release this clinging, yet you willfully continued. As these moments appear, release them to God's merciful, reconciling power.

3. What rises when you ask: "If I am granted further life here, how am I called to be present to God and others?" You may want to write down whatever comes in order to aid your memory.

REFLECTION

If you are in a group, share whatever you most need to remember, especially what rose in step three. Share your insights and questions about death, change, self-image, and God.

EXERCISE 19: POSSESSIONLESS JOURNAL KEEPING

When memories become too strongly attached to self-image they have a way of being very sticky. Instead of being held lightly in our experience, they become heavy and binding. As we have seen, they begin to overdefine us at the level of ego self-image in a way that draws our identity away from its depth in God. Among other consequences, this can lead us to fear death even more, because we have woven ourselves into such a vivid, separately defined possession.

Some kinds of journal keeping have a way of reinforcing this tendency. We write about our experience and ideas in a way that we reify a vivid, hard sense of self: "I" am and "I" do this and that. The defined "I" becomes an enlarged self-image with which we ultimately identify, and which we don't want to lose.

Writing can be done with a different intent, though: an intent to lighten the possessive "I" and remain close to the "I" in God. Conversion of our sense of self in memory and the present involves such a graced process. We need to remember here that European languages, unlike a number of others, condition us to a hard, possessive sense of "I." "I" as an isolated entity does not even exist in the vocabulary of some other languages (just as hard, linear distinctions between past, present, and future do not exist; both people and time are seen far more contextually).

1. Spend some time writing about experiences and insights as you might normally do in journal keeping, but with this difference: use no possessive pronouns. Instead of *I had a dream last night in which I was doing . . .*, write *Dream last night in which . . . happened.* As you are writing you may make insightful connections with other things. However, leaving out the extra mental step of possessing the experience with an "I" leaves room for it to just be experience and insight happening from which "I" is not separated out. Ego self-image, "I," is present assisting the reflection, but it is not the ultimate subject. Then your larger being in God is free to be manifest. That beingness has a calm, spacious, grounded-in-God quality.

Anything that may be called for out of the experience: particular actions, further insights, would come with a more uncalculating, not self-special simplicity, because it would not be mediated by a self-important sense of "I." Much action comes from such a sense of self-importance. The most called for actions, though, come from a more participative self. These are our "self-forgetful" actions, as when we pick up a dropped fork off the floor, or help someone without any sense of calculated effort: we just *do* it.

2. An even simpler way of writing in this mode would be in the form of very simple poetry, a genre of writing that draws on more directly participative than analytical awareness. For example, write in the style of Japanese *haiku,* which in one form would be restricted to a three-line poem with two accented syllables in the first line, three in the second, and two in the third.[3] As in step 1, use no possessive pronouns, or else, write with them once, and then a second time without them, noticing the difference. Here is an example by Ken Feit:

> Icicles and water—
> old differences dissolved . . .
> drip down together.

You will note a connection between this "simplification" of our sense of self and the simplification of feelings in exercise 12. In both cases the hard possessive "I" subject is being lightened. We are not left with less of a self, just less of a hard, possessive self-image that is disconnected from God and the situation.

RE-MEMBERING SCRIPTURE

We can bring to Scripture a very hard "I," one that feels it must get something out of it, find something to possess for itself, something to secure and give it a way of enhancing itself. The result is a dismemberment: God, "I," and world are defined apart. We can and usually do live that way, with many worthy results for us and others, but we will likely be living more of the Law than the Gospel. By that I mean we will live in hidden fear of losing that hard "I"; we will follow a moral way in part to preserve this "I"; we will rigidly cling to a secure belief that God will save my "I."

The word for *save* in New Testament Greek means "to make whole, to heal." From that word one of Jesus' titles is derived: "Sōtēr," Savior, Healer. So much that I have been saying in this book declares our wholeness to be in our identity with God. It cannot exist in the fragmented identity of self so supported by Western culture. God is our subject, in which we subsist, not our object out there. Ego self-image is a function of that larger reality. It exists as a dimension of a gifted self that does not ultimately belong to itself as an isolated entity, but belongs to God as an offspring.

When we open Scripture for prayer with this sense of self in God, we bring to it a different mind. It is a mind that seeks to lay on the page its tempting hard "I" to be cleansed in the fire of the Word. It opens to the One who sees behind our eye. The spaciousness of our identity in God rises and is fed through the words by the great loving spaciousness of God out of whom they rose, screened through the minds of the biblical writers.

In praying with Scripture in this way, our attention is not finally on grasping the words with our analytical minds, studying the historical and conceptual meanings. Beginning with such biblical study can be very helpful to our understanding, but our final aim is to move through the words into the awareness of the biblical author behind those words, before they became formed into meaningful images.

Those images could have been formed with a thousand different images in different cultures. But it is their shared Source we want to touch through them.

We want to be inside their liberating awareness of God firsthand, through which we can receive the Word that is meant for us, rather than forever being outsiders hammering at the door, guessing at the personal or corporate relevance of the author's words. We want to be *in* the mind of Christ! That is why we lay our constricted outside ego image on the page and let God "read" us into firsthand awareness. Perhaps this is related to what Isaac of Syria in the seventh century had in mind when he said that we must read the spaces as well as the words of Scripture. We cannot grasp the spaces. There our minds can only be in them, wide open, willing for God.

The words then can emerge as shapings of this spaciousness of God. They do not take us away from that shared spaciousness. They give it shape to enlighten and guide us now. We are not restricted to the historical images or the grasping of our outside minds. Our intent is to remain openly present through the words, as we are through the spaces, letting God shape our consciousness firsthand. The sections of Scripture that involve direct human-divine encounter best lend themselves to this way of being present to God. At those points Scripture can become a privileged stained glass window, through whose shapes God's light bathes us.[4]

EXERCISE 20: PRAYING WITH SCRIPTURE I: *LECTIO DIVINA*

The understanding of Scripture described in this chapter is adaptable to the classical *lectio divina* ("divine reading") way of praying with Scripture. It involves four steps, after an initial prayer for openness to God.

1. Begin with *reading,* stopping when a word or phrase really "shimmers," becoming a vibrant transparency of God for you. The intent is not to get to the end of a passage but to the bottom of it in God, to the word through which God touches you now, the word that becomes an icon for you. This is not always a strong awareness. Sometimes a word may shimmer only faintly, but enough to give you an obscure sense of God's presence through it.

2. Move toward an understanding of God in the word: the step of *reflection.* This step involves the use of your cognitive capacity to reflect on the possible spiritual meaning of the word for your life, and at times for the larger community's life. Do not try to force a meaning. This may not be clear. God is at work in you at a deep precognitive level, and you do not have to understand clearly what is happening. This will emerge as it is really important for you to know. Your steady trust and openness to God is more fundamental.

3. Move to active *prayer:* for your heart to open to God through this word in direct communion, and for your will to open to God in responsive action, as may be called for.

4. Finally, move to a *still presence* in the spaciousness of God. Seek

to simply rest in your larger identity in God, through and behind the images and feelings that may rise.

A rural Southern minister, not knowing this tradition technically but knowing it in his heart, summed it up succinctly when he was asked how he prays: "I read myself full, I think myself clear, I pray myself hot, and I let myself cool" (another version of his statement ends "let myself go").[5]

REFLECTION

1. If you are in a group, share the "word" that stopped you and what happened through the *lectio divina* process, unless you sense that what has been given you would be lost or diminished if you shared it aloud. You should note that the four steps need not be rigid. They may naturally flow in a different order. The contemplative presence of step 4, for example, may come and go between the other steps.

2. Share your ways and times of praying with Scripture, and its different mindset from *studying* Scripture.

3. What barriers to God's presence do you find in praying with Scripture (in yourself and in the words)?

4. How has God's presence surprised you through scriptural prayer?

EXERCISE 21: PRAYING WITH SCRIPTURE II: OTHER WAYS

In addition to *lectio divina*, this exercise gives three other ways of praying with Scripture.

1. The following is a simple *extension of "lectio divina"* (exercise 20), to be done either after step 4, or in place of steps 2 through 4. After a word (or phrase) has shimmered for you, stopped you, as though God is wanting to open you in some way through that word, just sit with it very simply. You might want to let it sit in your breath: seek to breathe in the word, without "stepping outside" it with your mind and directly struggling to grasp some meaning; let God quietly work in you through the word and give you whatever is called for. Breathe out with the intent of a trusting surrender to God, remaining still and open for a moment at the bottom of your breath.

This word can be taken with you through the day or week, becoming a transparency of God's presence for you. The Jesus Prayer[6] is an example of such a scriptural prayer, except that it is generalized for everyone. Even though it is not a unique word given to you, as in *lectio divina*, it is meant to be a means through which God uniquely "connects" with you.

Listening for such a shimmering word can be naturally extended to *all* your reading. You can remain open to the way God may shine through, in everything from the newspaper to novels to spiritual classics.

2. Another way to pray with Scripture is through the *repetitive reading of a passage*, with brief pauses between the readings. John Veltri tells of one form of this practice in an eighth-century Italian monastery, where a short Gospel passage of particular energy and color would be read over and over to the gathered monks until all were gone.[7] (Today we might perform this practice reading different translations of the passage each time.) As each monk sensed that he finally had been taken hold of by the passage, he left to pray over it in his cell. Perhaps the monk would have identified with some particular person in the passage through whom he was opened to his condition and God's presence.

The process involves letting the past become present through imagination and memory. Jesus and the event live here now in you. Your intent is to let your whole being become more vulnerable to the Spirit of the Living Christ working through the persons, words, and activities of the passage. For example, you may become identified with the blind Bartimaeus begging Jesus for sight (in Mark 10:46ff.) and in the process become more vulnerable to God's healing presence in your own life. You might eventually even find yourself spontaneously identified with Jesus, sensing the world through his eyes, his being in God, your being in God through and with him.

Try to let yourself open to an intimate presence for God through whatever images may appear in a particular passage. Eventually the images may dissolve, leaving a still, open presence for God.

3. Another form of biblical prayer draws on the *imagination* more precisely. Some people are able to image scenes in their minds much more easily than others. If this is difficult for you, then try to simply "sense" a scene's presence without worrying about trying to vividly picture it. Here is one form of this prayer. (a) Read some pictorial, dramatic passage twice (e.g., a healing story, ideally one with Jesus present), listening very openly. You might find yourself more fully present if you read to yourself or others out loud. (b) Close your eyes. See if you can join the scene with all your senses. Try to be fully present there with your senses of smell, taste, touch, hearing, and sight. (c) After a few minutes let the scene fade, except for you and Jesus. Try to be present as spontaneously as possible. You may want to ask or say something. You may be spoken to. You may do something or be silent together. Let it evolve as it will. If you notice any fear, resistance, or distraction, try to bring these to Jesus. (d) *An optional step:* on a sheet of paper, let that dialogue with Jesus continue in writing until it comes to a natural pause after a few minutes. Like a script, just write down the spontaneous dialogue as it unfolds. (e) Let the scene gently fade when the time seems called for. If possible let yourself move toward a simple sense of appreciation for God's grace at work in you through

the Living Christ, beyond any resistance or uncertainty you may have. (f) Try to open into a trusting, still presence, seeking to simply rest in your largest identity in God through whatever may rise in your mind.

REFLECTION

The questions suggested for exercise 20 can be easily adapted to these ways of praying with Scripture. More particularly you can note where you first found yourself in the scene, where you might have been led from there and what happened in your time with Jesus, and afterward. What does this say about your trust, openness, resistance, and sense of grace in Christ's presence?

When we approach Scripture with the mind I have described, and with a process such as I have suggested, God, self, and world are re-membered. The memories we may bring to scriptural prayer can participate in that re-membering as they appear, and our feelings as well. Indeed, we should bring to scriptural prayer as full and energetic a presence as we can, ready to "embody" the Word. Opening Scripture for prayer is like opening the door of our house. We can bring in everything that we are, in trust. The trust in God can be so full that we finally let go what we bring, until we stand naked, not even dressed in images. Then nothing is left standing between us.

CHAPTER 7

Acting

Acting, in the sense of bringing about change, is always happening in some form both in and around us. It is inherent to life. Here we will focus particularly on moral acts, which at their best are the overflow of God's love in and through us for the well-being of our neighbor in the most inclusive sense (i.e., our neighbor individually and corporately, friend and foe, human and in nature). Moral actions, too, are ceaselessly happening as God's pervasive love is circulated.

Authentic spiritual life, biblically and historically, has always held together the love of God, self, and neighbor. We see these side by side in Jesus' Summary of the Law:

You shall love the Lord your God with all your heart, and with all your soul, and with all your mind....You shall love your neighbor as yourself (Matt. 22:37-39, RSV).

The Hebrew scripture behind that last verse, found in Leviticus 19:17, can be translated as "love your neighbor as *the being of* yourself". If we combine this with the way Jesus speaks of us being *in* him and the Father (John 17:21), we see the incredible coinherence that is our starting point in reflecting on our neighbor. Jesus is constantly challenging us to see our inclusiveness as a community of mutual active caring.

Recent research has begun to give us a clearer neurophysiological basis for this larger caring. Paul MacLean speaks of the development of our cerebral cortex beyond reptilian and old mammalian capacities: "In creating for the first time a creature with a concern for all living things, nature accomplished a 180-degree turnabout from what had previously been a reptile-eat-reptile and dog-eat-dog world."[1]

Dr. Ralph Burhoe draws on concepts from physics, chemistry, biology and systems analysis to argue that religious rites, acts, and belief systems by their nature connect neurologically and resonate with the depths of the central nervous system. More specifically, he believes that religious information, interacting with the genetic information in our brains historically, led to our transformation into new creatures capable of altruism to strangers and civilized cooperation and self-giving. The self-denial shown by humans in building organizations, nations, and a global civilization cannot come from our selfish animal genes.[2]

Thus when we speak of spiritually forming our moral life, we are not speaking of imposing something alien to us, but rather of tapping into our deepest sensibilities. Unfortunately, as we all know, there is much in our mysterious willfulness and confusion that counters these sensibilities. We see the bitter fruits in the fourfold horror of our world: nuclear terror, personal and social oppression, environmental rape, and resistance to communion with God. This brokenness is compounded by what we would call the "natural" and "accidental" disasters: earthquake, flood, famine, disease, fire, physical death, and so forth. Such realities tempt us to numbness and escape. Who wants to face into so much suffering? Even if we do, what can we hope to accomplish?

At this point, our spiritual formation becomes crucial. We need to evolve the spiritual heart that is able to see through the surface of the suffering to the promise that is in us and in our world, revealed in Christ's suffering, death, and resurrection. We need to uncover our compassion, our particular gifts for active caring, and our called-for arenas of action. This uncovering emerges with our evolving conversion. As we more fully accede to God's life at the center of our own, the divine love that touches us begins to wear away the power of our own oppressive ego self-centeredness. In particularly graced times, this love can free us to see our own forms of constricted ego domination with particular force. Yet the pain of this awareness is offset by an overwhelming sense of God's acceptance that frees us from justifying the way we are. In effect, we experience repentance in such times.

One result of such repentance is to free God's love in us for others: for Godself, for people, and for the natural environment. Our normal ways of escaping and judging the messiness of the world are replaced or at least sidetracked by feeling the pain of what is happening and our desire for its relief. At our graced best we become vehicles of God's mercy. This can take several forms.

On the one hand, there is the direct caring we show for the victims of suffering (caused by themselves or by others). On the other hand there is our identification with God's vision for the world: the kingdom of heaven, *shalom*. We begin to recognize God at work in the world in often surprising and hidden ways (which we see throughout Scripture): in poor people (economically, mentally, physically, socially, or spiritually), peacemakers, children, ordinary work and human exchanges, collaborative ventures between recent enemies, and endless other outcroppings of divine-human collaboration. We find ourselves praying for these situations, and joining them as we are called.

DISCERNMENT

Trying to discern just how we are called to act amidst the myriad of opportunities and pressures usually is not easy. The historic practice of "discernment of spirits" rose out of the desire to sort out the movements within us: Which are of God? Which are of constricted ego forces (our own or others)? Which perhaps even are of demonic origin, perhaps disguised as "angels of light"?[3] There is a large literature in this subtle area and I cannot do it justice here.[4] In its fullness it goes beyond discernment of moral callings to include our callings to deeper direct communion; it can also simply involve an end-in-itself appreciation of God at work in me or us, without any sense of particular call at this time. I have already described a simple form of very general daily discernment in the Daily Examen exercise (page 84). Several points particularly related to contemplative formation, though, need to be mentioned here, following which I will offer a more particular exercise for discernment.

The purest discernment is the simplest. Sometimes we are such open channels of grace that we spontaneously say or do something for others that is completely uncalculated. It is only afterward that we realize by the fruits of our action that it was just what seemed called for. It may have been so uncalculated, so missing in any kind of self-image mediation, so self-forgetful, that we were not even aware that we had said or done anything of particular significance. One of the hopes of contemplative conditioning and its lightening of self-image centrality is that we might become such open channels of grace more frequently. I believe the anonymous author of *The Cloud of Unknowing* is speaking in this vein when he states that giving yourself "immoderately" to loving God in contemplative prayer can lead to a spontaneous capacity for spiritual discernment.[5]

Most of the time, however, discernment more likely will include a sense of self that is trying to note the pattern of God's invitations in our lives, in light of scriptural guidelines, personal and the larger Church's experience, and our particular gifts and situations, along with noting our areas of freedom and lack of freedom for God in our responses. A contemplative understanding, though, will distrust a too objective process for determining God's will for us. Once self-image mediation is involved, we are removed from an appreciative direct presence and prone to much guesswork influenced by much restrictive ego conditioning.

I do not think we can ever be absolutely certain of God's will for us through this process, even when the fruits seem good. However, such a process of discernment, especially as it honestly sifts through what may be of the false self rather than of God, holds out the hope of at least reflecting and reinforcing our *desire* for God's will, and this in itself will likely put us closer to it.

It is vital to remember the mystery of God's will to our constricted ego consciousness. Whatever it senses of God is mediated by our mental constructs so that we at best are "experiencing an experience" of God. Thus we need to be suspicious of our own and others' too glib comments about discernment. When we say or hear, "God told me to do this or that," we must carefully question where that discernment is coming from, how it was determined, and where it leads, for example, to greater or lesser compassion, self-importance, or defensiveness.

We especially need to notice our disposition during the discernment. Were we really open to move any direction that might be called for, or did we have an advanced vested interest in the discernment coming out one way or another? Were we honestly in touch with our areas that lack freedom, as well as those that have freedom, in responding? I suspect that a lot passes for discernment that really is pious justification for doing what we want (at least I know how capable of this I am!). It is a long road to the point where we genuinely trust that what God wants is really what we desire and what will be best for us (even if it means martyrdom). Until that time, we need to be careful about rationalizing what our constricted egos want as God's will. This does not mean that what God wants necessarily is contrary to what our ego consciousness wants. God's desire for us I believe is reflected in all of our desires, however dimly or distortedly.

As our conversion deepens, and our locus of ultimate identity shifts from ego self-image to its Source, we will become more capable of cocreating God's way. The more our being in God is embraced, the more our doing will reflect the image of God. The more we become aware of all true life's ground in God, the less likely we are to be kidnapped by the relative disunity and friction of the world: we will remember our fundamental unity, even with our enemies. Believing in that unity helps us to be free for God's ever-reconciling will.

EXERCISE 22: DISCERNING ACTION

Discernment of what is seemingly consonant with God's will in regard to a particular significant action being contemplated normally is a *process,* not a single step. The following is one way to *begin* this process:

1. Relax your body and mind in whatever way this best happens for you; for example, take a few long, slow breaths.

2. Be in touch with your desire for God's will. Ask that you be shown what you need to realize about that will as you and the situation are ready to receive it. You might find it helpful to envision yourself as

floating on God's sea. You are not in control of your direction and speed in the way of a swimmer; rather, as you float, you gently respond to the movements of wind and current. You are actively receptive.[6]

3. Place before God some area of your life where you feel an internal desire for action (for example, in regard to a particular social action, job, or a relationship). Notice the images, thoughts, and feelings that rise. Note their relation to your own ego desires and fears, and to any sense of God's desire for you. God's desire may become a little more apparent if you reflect on the pattern of recent actions in your life that seem to have brought you closer to God, and those that seem to have left you more distant. Note the possible consequences for yourself and others in moving one way or another, as well as their consonance with Christ's way as revealed in Scripture.

4. Now release yourself to God as best you can and be simply present with a quality of open, trusting awareness. Centering Prayer or its equivalent may help you here.

5. End with a surrender of your discernment process to God, asking that whatever action is taken be consonant with the divine will.

You may be moved to repeat this process a number of times in regard to a particular subject of discernment. You also may need to gather more data related to your discernment: discernment takes into consideration all relevant facts, with the backdrop of your faith-identity.[7] If eventually you sense a deep quality of peace for moving a particular direction (beyond any anxiety about some personal sacrifice or risk that may be involved), this may be a sign of the right time to take a step. However, you may never have any significant interior indications of what to do. Then you must take whatever step seems best, desiring it to be congruent with God's will. Remember that will always remain a mystery in part, but it will not be contrary to love as reflected, for example, in the fruits of the Spirit (Gal. 5:22), nor will it be contrary to your basic God-given nature.

It is possible that any number of courses of action may be consonant with God's will; action then is left to your God-oriented freedom. Keep in mind that the actions rising from your discretionary freedom may in fact not be distant from God, but rather an intimate expression of God's free Spirit uniquely immersed in you, a particular reflection of God's nature of freedom that you are privileged to share.

You may sense that no course of action is appropriate now. It is a time for patience. Reflection about this and other options along with the whole discernment process with a spiritual friend can be very helpful in avoiding self-deception and confusion, noticing the possible direction of God's will, and supporting your courage to act if called for.[8]

Remember the difference between this discernment process, which largely involves a sense of reflective self-image, and the "purer" direct actions mentioned earlier that happen beyond your calculation. Remain open for these, trusting that God does not always need our calculated cooperation. God's Spirit sometimes will blow best through our simple, childlike, unself-conscious, available presence.

PRESENCE TO GOD IN OUR WORK

Our work (whether in the form of gainful employment or voluntary service) is our ministry, whenever our intent is to share God's compassion or creativity. Even with this intent, though, it is a particularly difficult arena in which to attend God's presence. Our constricted ego presence tends to reign supreme. This is one reason for the historic weekly (and daily) rhythm of Christian time that moves between unambiguous presence to God in sabbath time and a more background presence to God during work time.[9] Without the conditioning given us in time devoted to unambiguous presence to God, our awareness would likely become even more remote from God during work time. Such remoteness cultivates an alienated, unjust, violent social environment.

CULTURAL BARRIERS TO CONTEMPLATIVE PRESENCE IN THE WORK WORLD

We need to be aware of some "built in" obstacles to practicing the presence of God that are found in Western, and many Eastern, cultural settings today. One of the primary barriers is the growing dominance of what Ivan Illich calls "economic man."[10] Such a person views happiness and self-esteem primarily as the result of personal material production and consumption, rather than as the result of a reflective and attentive life oriented to God. With a view of scarcity of material resources in relation to our needs and wants, prevailing cultural values press us to believe that we must continually gain more such resources. Of course, there is a minimum viable material standard that needs to be advocated for everyone, as well as a basic dignity to productive work and enjoyment of its fruits that needs to be supported. It is when we move beyond such rightful economic considerations to economic idolatry that we unnecessarily sentence ourselves to a life of hard labor.

In the process of increased efficiency and drivenness in our work and consumption, we lose our sense of intrinsic worth that sabbath time teaches. In the midst of controlling superefficiency in our work, we lose a sense of what seems like the "unproductive" spaces through which we can notice God's spacious, uniting presence.

Related cultural values also block contemplative ones. Heaven is ahead in contemporary culture: we work for a future reward. But heaven is already here in contemplative awareness (if not yet fully realized). The current moment is not empty and impoverished, something to be skipped over on the way to some idyllic future. God's presence is here now, everywhere. We are to live straight up in the present instead of just bent forward toward the future. Further, contemplative awareness values the process of working as a meaningful act in itself, part of our daily living in God, not just as a dead means to some supposedly live end product.

Finally, contemporary culture values growth, with its consequent complexity and bureaucratization. Contemplative presence values the reverse flow: to an inner and, where possible, outer simplicity. It values a personal littleness that is intent on penetrating to God's heart and our unity in things, rather than seeking to possessively dominate ever more fully whatever we can with our product, our institution, our constricted egos.[11]

SUPPORTING OUR PRESENCE TO GOD IN WORK

Given all the personal and cultural barriers to our God-presence during work, we need help for our attentiveness. Hopefully we can find someone to support us in caring about practicing the presence during our work, someone with whom we can look at the ways our own attitudes and practices veer away from and toward God's presence, and what we are called to do about these. This may be a spiritual friend, a workmate, or a small group of church people gathered to reflect upon, pray about, and mutually support one another in their various work settings.

The "base communities" (informal regular small gatherings of Christians for prayer, Scripture, and reflection on callings and actions) so prevalent in Latin America today are often fine current examples of such groups, though their focus usually is broader than work. Their frequent focus not only on personal understanding and support but on ways of helping the larger society to make the changes necessary to support more just and spiritually motivated values and structures is well worth heeding. The long history of American voluntarism: local organized initiatives for needed personal and social changes, is a positive legacy that can support the further formation of such groups in North America.

The church can be a place not only for attention to our work settings elsewhere, but also a setting where we can directly work on immediate church affairs while collectively practicing the presence together. This is a vital element of spiritual formation that can spill over into people's other work and service settings, where such attention is more difficult because others usually are not motivated to any collective attentiveness, unless it is a voluntary subgroup of concerned people meeting apart from others. Unfortunately such collective attentiveness is not the norm in many churches I know, and a precious opportunity is lost both for learning and for evolving decisions and actions that lean closely into God.

WORK AND PRESENCE AT SHALEM

In "work" sessions of the Shalem Institute over the years we have struggled to practice the presence in a variety of ways. I will share a few of these as a means of stimulating your imagination as to what might be called for in your own situations.

When we gather for administrative meetings (Executive Committee, Board of Directors, etc.), we explicity agree upon particular ways of helping us to remain attentive to God during the time. These ways emphasize silence. For example, we may begin a meeting with five or ten minutes of silence (depending on the meeting's length), ending with a prayer and possibly Scripture. Everyone connected with us has been given prior assistance with ways of being present to God during the silence, so it is not a perfunctory time to collect our thoughts for the meeting. Our intent is to condition us to want to listen more deeply than our own thoughts to the true Guide of the meeting, and to give our minds a spacious environment that can help that listening.

Once we move into the business at hand, there is a great temptation to leave God behind and let our constricted egos come in, not as expedient servants but as ultimate arbiters of the truth. Something in us wants to take over, get on with it, and get our way. It can be a great ascetical practice to withstand such temptations and submit ourselves to the mystery at hand, remaining open for the surprises of the Spirit as they may show themselves through one another, and retaining a patiently discerning mind concerning what may be of God and what may be of other forces in us and others.

Such collective patience is difficult when we have been conditioned to the priority of the individual over the group in our society. We usually find collective patience best illustrated in such Christian subcultures as the Quakers (The Society of Friends), the Mennonites, and vowed religious communities (such as the Jesuits), who have evolved their own ways of God-centered collective decision-making.[12] I recall a Mennonite overseer once telling me how much he looked forward to corporate meetings, because he trusted that the Spirit would show itself whenever "two or three are gathered together."

In Shalem business meetings, we have tried to assist our resistance to personal and corporate "ego takeover" in several ways. Sometimes we will ask for volunteers to pray for fifteen minutes each during the meeting. They remain physically present but quiet during the agreed upon time. It is amazing what effect this can have on everyone. For the individuals praying, they can notice the relinquishment of ego control in offering the group to God and sense their capacity to be valuable to the group not through their insights but through humble intercession. For the group, the person's silent presence can powerfully symbolize the group's dependence on God's will and the desire of the group to align itself with that will beyond its narrow ego fears and desires.

Over time there is always the danger of routinizing a particular way of praying, so that its capacity to really assist the group's presence to God is diminished. In order to avoid this, we have varied the way we pray during meetings from time to time. For example, we might all stop for five minutes of prayer every half hour during the meeting (no matter where we are in our deliberations), or for two minutes every twenty minutes. Everyone has the right to ask for a moment of silence at any time, which has been very helpful when we have found ourselves in conflict, confusion, or collective willfulness. However, we need to be careful that the silence not become an instrument of the false self, used as a way of squelching valid dissent or otherwise becoming manipulative.

Such practices and attitudes during meetings have been vital to our ongoing discernment of what is called for. Like all religious organizations today, we are subject to constant pressures for decisions about far-reaching matters. Among these are concerns about mission: what we are uniquely called to at this time, where, and how; about money: how much is needed, how to distribute it fairly, how to raise it carefully; about staff: who do we need doing what; about property: how to be good stewards of our space and equipment; about the relations and work of men and women and other groupings as they affect issues of justice and mission; and about one another: how to deal with our differences with mutual respect, constructive challenge, forgiveness when called for, and seeking God's will through careful mutual listening.

One of the fruits of our attempts to be careful about God's place in our discernment has been to free us to let discernment be a process over time rather than a final product needed today. Our ego desires are usually ahead of what is really called for and time is needed to let what is called for appear. We have found almost invariably that slowing down our discernment has led to a better decision, with more people having a sense of rightness about it than would ever have been possible otherwise. Of course, in some organizations there is the opposite danger of moving slower than the Spirit may be inviting. If the people involved are genuinely caring about alignment with God's will, though, hopefully their own ego resistance will be relinquished in due time.

The spiritual formation task in this arena is to provide an environment that sensitizes us to the difference between our constricted ego desires and fears and our deeper caring about God's will, and to encourage our willing relinquishment to the latter rather than our justification of the former, when there is a clash. Such an environment can nourish the prophetic seedbed of the church's life, and of the members' lives of work and service in other places.

HABITUAL PRAYER

Let's look more precisely now at the quality of spiritual consciousness we need during work time. When our minds are fully occupied with particular tasks, God is absent to our minds in the sense of direct awareness. Yet we can retain a background awareness of God in our hearts. This may be characterized by a generalized sense of spaciousness, an even-minded background of grace in which we abide through whatever we may be doing. What we are doing is not apart from this background. Rather, our doing is suffused with the being of grace.

We are not further dividing our awareness by trying to rememeber God as well as the work situation we are in, but just the reverse. Our spiritual heart is revealing the radiant unity of self, work situation, and God that our working minds easily forget. We are recovering the sanity of our given wholeness and relativizing the insanity of our minds' constant tendency to split reality into ultimate pieces. This quality of background presence to God is *habitual prayer:* our habitual openness to grace through the active day, "praying constantly" (1 Thess. 5:17).

Without this quality of presence to God through our work, we are more likely to become idolatrous. As the gate to that presence is locked from our side, we are left with the fears and ambitions of our constricted ego consciousness as ultimate rather than relative to a deeper, trustworthy, guiding Mystery. We then are more prone to work with either too much self-confidence (insisting on getting our way), or too little self-confidence (afraid that we cannot work effectively, always worrying about how we are doing). We become centered in ourselves or in the group, because we have shut out our larger being in God.

I believe this potential narrowing of life, with all its personal and social consequences, lies behind Jesus' exhortation to be *in* the world but not *of* it, that is, to be in the world but of *God,* capable of discerning and carrying out actions that are aligned with God in intent.[13] The house built by our actions then will be built on rock rather than on sand; it will more likely be a temple of the Spirit, than of illusory ego fluff. Habitual prayer, suffused with our desire for God through all things, is what we can do from our side to assist such openness to God through our work.

EXERCISE 23: HABITUAL PRAYER: ATTENTION TO GOD THROUGH OUR WORK

What helps us remain attentive to God through our work can vary a great deal from person to person. We need to pray about what form may be best for us and notice what actually assists our presence to God. Whatever it is should not interfere with the quality of our work. Indeed, the quality may be enhanced as we become less deflected by our constricted ego pressures. But our intent in habitual prayer should not be greater efficiency in our work. Rather, at its best it will be motivated by our desire for *kenosis,* for emptying of self-inflation, that we might share the mind of Christ that lives out of God. "[He] emptied himself, taking the form of a servant" (Phil 2:7). Then we will be free to let God work through our work.

This exercise suggests four ways to pray through your workday.

1. If you find Centering Prayer (exercise 5) particularly helpful to your presence for God, you might find the word you use in that prayer helpful during your work. As you begin your work, gently bring the word to mind and see if you can let it rest just beneath your consciousness. During your work you would not normally be directly aware of the word, but let your intent be for its hidden presence to keep your work open to God's spacious presence. In moments of particular temptation to become kidnapped by narrowing and destructive self-centered feelings, thoughts, or acts, you might let the word lightly rise to consciousness as a means of returning to your deeper desire for God.

2. Rather than your Centering Prayer word, you might find that a different word or phrase is better for you, perhaps one from Scripture. This might be used more consciously through your working day as a kind of mantra, lightly being repeated (without thinking about it) in the background of your mind. See if you can let this word carry your intent to give yourself to God through your work.

3. You might prefer or add a nonverbal form of habitual prayer. For example, you can attempt to let physical forms, sounds, touches, or smells be reminders of God's presence, so that you are freeing attention to God through one or more of your senses. You could also let your breath be a reminder of God. Do not concentrate heavily on the form itself. The form is only a vehicle of your will for God. Just let it quickly draw you to an inclusive sense of presence. Let your ultimate intent be to restore your immediate vulnerability to God.

4. Your work itself might become a direct reminder of God. You can immerse yourself in it with the intent of surrendering to God in the process. You may be able to do this with a gentle, simple, unpossessive, very present directness. This can weaken a complicated, worrisome mind that pesters you with such questions as: "Am I doing this right?" or "What will the results be?"

REFLECTION QUESTIONS

1. What are some major things in your work situations that draw you away from God? (Remember that *work situations* refer to all the times of work and service in your life, with other people or alone.)

2. What have you found most helpful in assisting your attention to God in various work situations?

3. Give some examples of how God seems to have been revealed *to* you and *through* you in various work situations.

4. Do you sense any particular calling to take the initiative to change the conditions of your work environment, or that of others, so that God might be attended more readily? (This can include work situations with others who share your desire for such attentiveness, such as in some church group. It can also include secular situations where you can more indirectly assist the environment for openness to God, e.g., through advocacy of a slower, more humane pace of work, or through bringing about a more just work situation. Injustice is always a diversion from God and cries out for our action.

INTERCESSION

Intercessory prayer for others is a fundamental form of action. It is one of the many privileged ways of acting that results from our being "in Christ," "in God." Out of that contemplatively realized unity grows our mysterious capacity to participate in the circulation of grace through the great cosmic Body of Christ.

Along with encouraging our intercession, Scripture offers certain guidelines for it. Following certain emphases from the Wisdom literature of Hebrew scripture, we find such exhortations as these: "Ask with faith and no trace of doubt" (James 1:6, JB, a theme implied often in the Gospels); "[do not] pray for something to indulge your own desires" (James 4:30, JB); "the heartfelt prayer of a good person works very powerfully. Elijah was a human being like ourselves, [and when he prayed earnestly he was answered]" (James 5:16-17, JB); "Whatever we ask [God] we shall receive, because we keep his commandments and live the kind of life that he wants" (1 John 3:22, JB); "we are quite confident that if we ask [God] for anything, and it is in accordance with his will, he will hear us" (1 John 5:14).

St. Paul consoles us about the confusion we may feel in intercession: "The Spirit helps us in our weakness; for we do not know how to pray as we ought, but the Spirit [itself] intercedes for us with sighs too deep for words" (Rom. 8:26). Such words express the incredible intimacy of God's Spirit and our own, our unity in diversity, and the preeminence of God's movement in us. We do not prayerfully intercede as an autonomous act of little ego. We intercede as vessels of the Spirit's intercession, reaching through us for the care and transformation of creation. That is the mysterious way in which God seems to have made life, a way in which we have a part.

Accepting the invitation to intercessory prayer helps to condition us to see and accept the invitation to intercessory action in other forms.

Indeed, one of the dispositions for authentic intercession is our willingness to participate in any called-for actions that rise from our prayer. Scripture forever looks to the fruits of compassion in our lives as signs of our truly living our of God's love. But, like intercessory prayer, such fruits do not grow out of an attempted autonomous action, but out of a desire for God's will to be done.

Intercessory prayer can happen in many forms. Exercise 24 offers a way that tries to keep it close to God.

EXERCISE 24: INTERCESSION

1. Ask for your own openness to God's Spirit.

2. If you want to include petitions for yourself at this point before moving to intercession for others, let them be just as honest as you can. Let your true desires surface and be offered into your deepest desire for God's will to be done.

3. Let people and situations spontaneously rise to your awareness. With or without particular words, offer them to God, remembering the partiality of your understanding and your ultimate hope for God's loving will to be done, whatever that may be. Be open for the inclusion of enemies, ethnic and racial groups, nations, and the natural environment. Be especially open for victims of various kinds of oppression and your sense of God's and your unity with them.

4. Remain a while with an open presence, inviting the Spirit to pray through you beyond your conscious intercessions, "with sighs too deep for words."

5. Ask that you be made aware of any particular called-for actions on behalf of those for whom you have prayed.

6. Say the Lord's Prayer (silently or aloud) very slowly, pausing between each phrase.

7. End with a simple sense of confidence in God.

REFLECTION QUESTIONS

1. What seem to be the effects of such prayer on you, the pray-er?
2. Does God's power and yours seem to be the same or different in your prayer? *Who* is praying?
3. If a particular person, group, or situation does not appear in your prayer spontaneously, what may be the reason?
4. If you are sharing in a group: What are some of your experiences and questions around intercessory prayer?

MONEY

Each of us takes our place in God's world day by day with our particular gifts, space, time, prayer, and energy for survival and for service. Each day we find ourselves receiving these goods from others. Through these dimensions of mutual presence we circulate God's grace among us. Spiritual formation includes attention to each of these through regular reflection, ideally with a spiritual friend. Part of this reflection needs to include our attitude toward money. Since this is often the last area that people want to directly associate with the spiritual life, let me spend some time bringing it into the orbit of the holy.

For a number of years now Shalem has sponsored workshops on the subject of money and spirituality. We were originally inspired by the work of Don McClannen, a member of the ecumenical Church of the Savior in Washington, D.C., who began an organization called "The Ministry of Money." Its logo is a cross with a dollar sign through it. If you react negatively to that, my guess is that you have some trouble dealing with money and spirituality. Most of us do. Scripture is aware of our trouble: money, according to Don, is the second most talked-about subject in the Bible. Probably it is the most talked-about subject in Western societies, and in many other societies as well.

It is one of those subjects that particularly sticks to our little egos. The more separate we believe ourselves to be, or want to be, the more important money is likely to become: to secure and enhance our independence and control. The increasingly dominant and commercially pressed values of "economic man," earlier described, reinforce such a tendency. It we have some social conscience, we are likely to oscillate between narcissism and guilt. Money has a particularly powerful way of bringing out of us some of those classic deadly sins, such as greed, envy, avarice, sloth, and pride, sins that veer our desires away from God and our true self, as well as injure our neighbor.

As a result of these many "weights" around money, we probably would just as soon bury the subject when we come to God. It often is one of those things we would rather not bring to prayer (ritualized exhortations to do so during the annual church stewardship campaign not withstanding). But money in itself is neutral. Like anything else in our lives, it can be an idol that enslaves, deflects, and destroys, or it can be an icon through which God blesses us, an energy of God that we are called to appreciate and circulate with joy. Scripture shows both of these potentials in many ways. As we have seen, money is a particularly powerful energy in human hands. It can take us over and become a substitute for God. The Aramaic root of "mammon" used in The Gospels according to St. Luke and St. Matthew means "to trust in." Mammon competes with God for our ultimate trust. As Jesus said, we cannot finally serve both (Matt 6:24). Money must be tamed and channeled for the benefit of creation. Martin Luther once said that we all need a special conversion of the purse (echoing many others back to Jesus himself).

Once this conversion is accomplished, however, money can be seen as a gift that comes to us and passes to others, as needed for serving God's Reign on earth. When it passes from us to a sacrificial degree it takes an act of trust to believe that what we need will come to us through others. The more we have experienced a supportive community with God and other people, the easier such trust will be. Given the nature of human withholding in an individualistic society, though, and the vagaries of our economic systems, most people feel the prudent need for a certain amount of reserve, even if only in the form of an annuity fund for their old age. Few people living above the poverty line find themselves with the full interior freedom and external circumstances that would support a call to voluntary poverty, though we need to be open for such a call if it comes (See Luke 18:18-25). All of us, however, are drawn to a certain simplicity as our spiritual life deepens, not only for moral reasons, but also because we have seen through the happiness myth of "economic man."

For me this happens most clearly when I am in the midst of meditation. As I relinquish my surface striving to God, I become aware of the great richness that is present all the time. I am aware of a sufficiency of real wealth, which is not inherently connected with material wealth, since it costs nothing. This awareness leaves me a little more free to lighten my attachment to money. I realize its practical necessity and value in human life, but I need not make more of it than it is. I become a little easier in receiving it and passing it on where needed. I am able to be committed to its just distribution as part of God's vision, but I am clear that it is penultimate to God's *shalom*, not the content of it. Money is one more expedient form of energy through which God's care can be seen and shared—no more, no less.[14]

EXERCISE 25: BRINGING MONEY TO PRAYER

1. Relax your body and mind.
2. Ask in prayer that you may hear what you need to hear about the ways money is an idol and an icon in your life through your slow reading (or hearing) of two or more of the following biblical passages.

Exod. 20:13,15,17; 1 Chron. 29:14; Matt. 6:24-25,32-33; Luke 18:18-25; Luke 19:1-10,12-26; Luke 12:16-21 (or Matt. 6:19-21); 2 Cor. 8:9

After each passage, write down whatever comes to mind, including any feelings, and positive and negative examples from your own life.

3. Reflect on your life of prayer. How does money enter your prayer? How has prayer affected your feelings about money? Do you notice any change in your attitudes as your relation to God has changed over time?

4. From your reflection in steps 2 and 3 above, do you sense any particular calling now in the ways you can open money to God in your attitude and action? Be very quiet and open as you listen. Your answer may evolve over time with this discernment. As something does come with a sense of rightness and peace, commit yourself to follow that call. Whether or not something comes, commit yourself to keep money open to God in your prayer.

5. Now for a few minutes stop your reflection and just be open to God. Offer up very simply any insights, fears, concerns, or hopes related to money that may be lingering in your mind. Try to rest in trust of God as your deepest security, power, and happiness. End with a prayer that you be empowered to let money be a material energy of God's love which you can freely circulate with joy, as you are called.

THE ASCETICAL VALUE OF COMPASSIONATE ACTION

Our actions in the worlds of work and service not only serve God in our neighbor, they also serve God in ourselves. Very practically, as the Trappist Thomas Keating puts it,

[Compassionate service to others] neutralizes the deep-rooted tendency to become preoccupied with our own spiritual journey and how we are doing.... [Such service, in combination with dedication to God], is the indispensable means of stabilizing the mind in the face of emotionally charged thoughts [arising during contemplative prayer], whether of self-exaltation or self-depreciation.[15]

Our attempts to actively care for the world also provide a testing ground for the depth of our dedication to God. Again and again I have found my own dedication challenged by personal attachments that become transparent in the midst of various kinds of actions in the world. I also have found the limits of my own willful ego as I try too hard to make things happen. I continue to learn personal humility and reliance on God's mercy in ways that no other situations could teach. On the lighter side, I learn more about the unity and generosity that reflects God's way in and among us. As Paul Gorman and Ram Dass put it,

Each time we seek to respond to appeals for help we are being shown where we must grow in our sense of unity and what inner resources we can call upon to do so. We are constantly given, for example, the chance to experience the inherent generosity of our heart. Each time this happens, our faith in that part of ourselves which is intimately related to the rest of the universe is strengthened.[16]

Despite its many difficulties, I think we can see the normal necessity of gainful employment (as opposed to voluntary service) as a gifted arena for the development of such spiritual self-knowledge. Having to earn a living (as opposed to earning heaven) forces us to "stay in there" with the world of people and exchange of necessities, through which God teaches us, like it or not. I am including homemakers in this arena, since the steady demands of children and family, and the structures of the world into which they lead us, make this a major and crucial arena of work.

Thus we see that in many ways the world of human moral action is a fundamental arena of the spiritual life. God is revealed there, and calls us further into sharing divine compassion and the shaping of life. And we are revealed there, in all our amazing giftedness, limitation, and reliance upon God's mercy. As Beatrice Bruteau says in broadest perspective: "If one is united to God then one must do what God does, and what God does is to be endlessly self-expressive (as well as self-uniting) in the Trinity, and create the world."[17]

CHAPTER 8

Appreciating

Not long ago I found myself looking out my bedroom window for no particular conscious reason. In the midst of admiring the beauty of the spring trees and birds nesting in them, I was suddenly overwhelmed with the precious gift that appeciation is. God did not have to make us capable of such appreciation. We could just as easily have been made robot-style, moving about utterly unappreciative of life forms. But that would have been a contradiction of our intended nature.

More than anything else our capacity for multileveled appreciation sets us off from the rest of nature as we know it. At the same time it witnesses to our coinherence with other living forms. We are able to appreciate because we recognize brothers and sisters, or at least distant cousins, everywhere we turn, and we are made in such a way that we are attracted to them, or at least curious about them. St. Francis knew what he was talking about when he addressed sister moon and brother wolf. We mysteriously belong together in this creation, and our endlessly dynamic interweaving is full of wonders.

The deeper our surrender to God, the more the wondrous nature of life appears. No wonder the words for *confession* and *praise* are the same in both Hebrew (*yadah*) and Greek (*homologeo*) scripture: one leads to the other. When we confess our needless separation in the face of God's revealed love and desire for us, we shed the ultimate power of our grasping, fearing, controlling false self which cuts us off from real appreciation. We are free to recognize life as an end-in-itself overflow of God's joy. Its beauty and ultimate unity appear everywhere. What else can we more validly do then than express our appreciation through praise of our shared mysterious Lover? Christian history is filled with countless examples of the power of this appreciation even in the face of the worst external human conditions and threats. Many have learned with St. Paul that nothing external can separate us from the love of God shown us in Christ (Rom. 8:35).

We know great pain when the false self reappears and eclipses our appreciation of life in God, because we have tasted the truth. Our pain

is deepened as we see what happens to the world when that appreciation never appears, or is buried too long and replaced by the fearful
stridency and discord of that false self. We weep with Jesus then over
the Jerusalem that clings to its impoverished littleness amidst the available richness of our true selves and community in God.

The spiritual life, our true human life, begins with the dim desire
for this richness. It matures with its appreciation and sharing. Its various mysterious stages are divine gifts from start to finish. And yet in
our freedom we are able to reject the gifts, and in our ignorance and
distraction to miss or distort them. Thus we come to realize the value
of careful spiritual formation that helps to sensitize us to what is being
laid in our lap by God in endless ways. Formation in appreciation is
no exception.

MOVING FROM SELF TO GOD-APPRECIATION

Appreciation is a natural gift. It is meant to lead us to God. But it
may lead us just to self. Most commercial advertising assumes that we
want our appreciation to be little—self-centered: what we can gain from
life in terms of power, control, security, and self gratification.

On a practical ego level these things may be quite appropriate within
limits. For example, if we have the opportunity of taking a vacation
somewhere, we would like it to be a place that is relatively secure from
various serious dangers and provides an environment that allows us to
do various things for which we have skill, and enjoy. In other words,
we would like it to be a situation that enhances our capacity to appreciate life insofar as our senses allow. That is the most universally shared
understanding of appreciation. It is where we begin as human beings.
But it does not reflect the fullness of our calling.

A restlessness that is of God remains in us, however dimly. We may
mistake this to mean that our ego gratification needs still further stim-
ulation. Perhaps if we can manage to move to that vacation spot all will
be well. We want to possess a permanent place there and force-feed
ourselves with every pleasure we can. And make the place more secure.
And work harder to earn more money so that these things can happen.
On and on our confused egos strategize for the perfectly possessed
little—self-centered world.

Out of the continuing restlessness and ultimate emptiness of such
attempts, or before we even try very hard, we hopefully will be moved
in another direction. Instead of trying so hard to possess and cling to
what we appreciate, we can relax our striving and let ourselves be possessed by the One who gives the beauty. We can let the beauty lead us
to that wondrous Presence. There is nothing to possess then. Our center no longer is our grasping ego consciousness. Beauty becomes a dimension of the very nature of life in God. It no longer is a thing to

be possessed, a scarce commodity to be touched occasionally. It is the inherent quality of everything known in God. Our own souls and creation's soul shine with the radiance of the One whose light bears them into being and endless transfiguration.

Appreciation naturally appears the moment our self-concern is relinquished. It cannot be possessed and it cannot be earned; it simply *is*, a free gift, available everywhere. Life is known then more as art than task. The greatest task becomes our work to help others realize such wonder. The wonder is so great that we are in danger of overfascination. We easily become focused on the gifts as an end in themselves; they do not always lead us to the Giver. We subtly become attached to the felt beauty and miss not only the initial invitation to thanksgiving, but the yet deeper invitation: to release ourselves to God as we are enabled and let rise that full quality of awareness that is beyond felt beauty, beyond self-reflective appreciation.

Our valuation of this quality of presence, where theologically we might say we are fully hid with Christ in God (Col. 3:3), frees us from stridently seeking or clinging to moments of reflective appreciation. We no longer look for the appreciative "highs" as though they are the pinnacle of human spiritual awareness. Indeed, they are the pinnacle of spiritual *experience*, that is, the height of our self-reflective capacity to be in conscious touch with the holy. We can appreciate these times as they come. But our contemplative intent is to be released through them to God. When we are graced to do this fully, our self-definition, our reflective sense of self, if present at all, is but the thin surface of an inclusive awareness without special content, an empty fullness. This I believe is a participation in God's awareness, insofar as humanly possible: the greatest privilege, of literally being made in the image of God.

John of the Cross describes this God-given awareness at its transforming height with the analogy of light in a crystal:

When light shines upon a clean and pure crystal, we find that the more intense the degree of light, the more light the crystal has concentrated within it and the brighter it becomes; it can become so brilliant due to the abundance of light it receives that it seems to be all light. And then the crystal is undistinguishable from the light, since it is illumined according to its full capacity, which is to appear to be light. . . . God's love [has] arrived at wounding the soul in its ultimate and deepest center, which is to transform and clarify it in its whole being, power, and strength, and according to its capacity, until it appears to be God.[1]

This awareness finally is extremely simple and plain. There is nothing of "us" left to complicate it. And yet we are not destroyed. Our expedient, reflective little self is suspended; our "deepest center" in God is revealed. This is appreciation beyond appreciation — our participation in the Source of appreciation, before our consciousness divides and becomes self-reflective and says: "I" am here appreciating that beautiful flower, which draws "me" to God.

Both levels of appreciation are part of our gifted humanity that can reveal God. One is more mediated, one is more direct. In an embryonic, not yet fully graced way, perhaps they flow together all the time when we look precisely at what is happening. Before we begin our commentary on the beauty of something, and its Source, we simply are part of the beauty. We are "in" it. We do not possess it, because a sense of "I-ness" has not yet risen. We are "not two" in that flash of presence. But then our consciousness moves to grasp the beauty, to identify something as beautiful and of God. In order to do this we must separate out an "I" and become two, at least expediently.

AIDS TO GOD-APPRECIATION

As God deepens in us, appreciation of life in God naturally flows. But since this can be so easily hidden in an unsupportive environment and amidst our little self's attempts to reclaim centrality, we need to be open to whatever might assist our appreciation.

LIFE AS ART AND TASK

First of all we need to assure ourselves a rhythm of sabbath and ministry in our lives (see chapter 7). Without unambiguous times in the week and day when we are free to just appreciate the giftedness of life, to recognize ourselves as intrinsically loved creations of God's joy, we will likely smother our capacity to simply appreciate life in God as an art and narrow ourselves to life in God as a task. Even during our tasks, wherever possible, we need to leave spaces to turn to God and simply appreciate the life in and around us.

Our work and service at its best will grow out of this appreciation. Even our hard work for social justice in the face of ugly, enduring resistance needs to be rooted in such appreciation. Christian service historically has been grounded in thanksgiving to God for redemptive life. It is a response to our sense of unity in God, an overflow of the compassion we know in God. That is a very different motivation for service than hatred or fear of some opposing person or group. Being human, such negative emotions will rise in us when we come up against brutality or other forms of oppression, but they need to be waves of feeling that are caught up and transformed in our deeper love.

Such love carries with it a deep trust that in the end God's way will prevail. I saw such trust incarnate in Archbishop Desmond Tutu of South Africa in a speech delivered during one of his early visits to the United States. Overflowing with a sense of unextinguishable joy and trust, he made it plain that the last word in South Africa would be God's word. His appreciation of God could not be finally eclipsed by those who are causing so much human suffering. His appreciation shone like a fire in that audience and spread itself among those present. Such publicly proclaimed appreciation thus serves the larger community's right motives just by being itself. The Good News is seen and action finds its true roots.

A very different example points to our need to remember appreciation in the face of death (a subject I have addressed in chapter 6). An inner city priest went to the home of a poor old lady in his parish. She was dying. When the priest came to her side, she said, "Don't talk and don't run." She seemed to want to die fully appreciative of her life in God, which was too deep for any consoling words at that point. And she wanted to die appreciative of the human community that incarnates God's presence on this plane of existence, which was too deep for words but not for silent, prayerful human presence. That is contemplative dying. It also becomes a reminder to us of our need to be appreciative of God's presence in the poor and otherwise "overlooked" people in the world. It was them who best responded to God through Jesus.

We can approach all of the myriad little ego deaths, all the ways we don't get what we want (as opposed to what we need) in our lives, in the same way as that woman faced physical death. These deaths hurt. But they are also opportunities to loosen attachments and free an appreciative presence to God and one another that is more than words can convey. Gregory of Nyssa in the early Church once said that concepts create idols, only wonder comprehends anything. We need to leave room for the silence that can free the wonder, as well as for the words.

A certain kind of wonder can release the creativity in us that becomes a blessing for others as well as ourselves. It is astounding what is shaped through us: music, forms, colors, words, movements, scientific experiment, and so on. We need to appreciate the marvel of this way we share God's nature as creator and let it lead us to praise, and at its fullest to God's cocreating with us, through us.

PLAYFUL CELEBRATION

Elsewhere I have spoken of the great value of authentic play, laughter, and celebration, including eucharistic celebration, for an appreciative presence.[2] Play and laughter can be especially helpful in attuning us to the surprising nature of grace that bursts through our attempts to overcontrol and predict life. They are light and free us from the heavy traps of our logic and attachments. Our imaginations are opened and our unique forms of creativity soar. We might even find a fresh capacity for forgiveness and the resulting reunion that reflects God's way. At their graced height, play and laughter find us and God united in the act, beyond conscious distinction.

Eucharistic celebration, when we don't work too hard at it but let it flow through us together, brings all the seeming pieces of life before us and shows them whole in God. It is thus no accident that Jesus and the early Church established this distinctive form of collective prayer as central to Christian practice and appreciation. It encapsules all that we are and all that life is, not just in words, but in a corporate act that presses beyond the adequacy of any words to interpret. We reenact in faith our reconciled unity in God through Christ in the living power of the Spirit. With word, gesture, and communing acts our reflective consciousness does the best it can to show forth the nature of life in God, always pointing us beyond itself to the mystery of our actual communion.

The Holy Eucharist, Holy Communion, Lord's Supper, or whatever else our traditions may call it, is a major school of spiritual formation that serves our life in God and with one another through all its stages. Affective relations with others are sharpened, heightening an awareness of community; the words help to interpret and guide our experience; the dialectic revealed between God and persons in the words and homily teach listening and response to callings; periods of silence teach contemplative presence; praising teaches praise; confession teaches responsibility and forgiveness.

Further, the collection teaches about a shared community of goods; the physical exchange of peace (or handshake) teaches reconciliation; the celebrative quality teaches an intrinsic value to life in God as well as the goodness of God; active participation reflects incorporation into a covenant and into the Mystical Body of Christ, and our need to actively embrace God and community; consecration of the bread and wine show the material and spiritual held together as one interdependent reality, in the context of sacrificial dying and trusting new life to rise with Christ.[3]

EXERCISE 26: GIVING THANKS

Thanksgiving to God is a significant theme in Jesus' life and teaching, thanksgiving with a humble heart. The Psalms frequently focus on praise and thanksgiving. St. Paul speaks of giving thanks to God in all circumstances (1 Thess. 5:18). Our temptation to false autonomy, for taking the ultimate credit for what happens, needs the antidote of frequent praise. So does our tendency to miss the grace subtly proffered us in so many events of our lives.

This exercise gives you one way to open youself to God through praise. As you pray in this way, you might remember the warning of the medieval mystic John Ruusbroec: "Those who do not praise God here on earth will remain without the power of speech in eternity."[4]

You might also remember the promising words of the contemporary Welsh poet, Bobbi Jones: "The most sound, complete, joyful thing we can do is praise God."[5]

1. Raise your open hands to shoulder height (the traditional Hebraic, and frequently used Christian prayer posture). Loosely hold them there as you take several long, slow breaths, opening your trust of God through all that is given.

2. Share the praise of one of the Psalms, such as 145 or 148, keeping your hands raised if it feels right to you as you speak, chant, or listen to it.

3. Now remain in silence for about ten minutes. As anything comes to mind, simply say, "thank you, God (or Lord)", and gently release it. Let this be your response to absolutely everything that appears to your consciousness, including judgments, images, resistance, confusion, sin, thoughts, and sounds. Do not *try* for anything to come. Just be present in open appreciation of God in all that does come. Be thankful even for the "nothing" *between* what comes (then there is nothing left standing without praise between you and God). Keep in mind that St. Paul said to be thankful *in* all things, not *for* all things. Your thanks is not meant to cover over bad things in your life that call for resistance. Rather, your thanks is your way of recognizing that God can bring good even out of the worst things, so there is no need for evasion or despair about anything.

You may want to prolong this time, letting yourself become more and more silent, and your thanksgiving more and more a wordless appreciative presence.

4. If you are in a group (or perhaps even if you are alone) you may want to sing a simple song of praise, such as an "Alleluia." You also may be moved to include more physical expressions of praise, such as swaying and other movements.

REFLECTION QUESTIONS

1. What was the impact of your thanksgiving on those things that appeared, and on your appreciation of God?
2. What is the place of thanksgiving and praise in your life, and what have been some of its effects?
3. What are some aids and barriers to your appreciative presence?

JOY AT THE CENTER

> "These things I have spoken to you, that my joy may be in you, and that your joy may be full." (John 15:11)

Thus does Jesus declare the centrality of joy in the spiritual life. St.

Paul calls it one of the gifts of the Spirit (Gal. 5:22). It is not the same as sensual pleasure which remains little—self-centered, narrowly exciting, and without fruit for the soul and community. Joy by comparison is God-centered, calmly expansive of the spiritual heart, potentially present regardless of external circumstances (including physical, mental, and social suffering), and full of appreciation for creation. At its graced fullness there is no longer a possessor or giver of joy, there is just a pervasive, unrestricted awareness that *is* joy.

Such awareness reflects our very existence as an unmerited overflow of God's joy. Like yeast rising, God's heart seems to continually swell with joy and burst into creation that "at heart" is made of that joy. The joy is marred by a resistant darkness, but by its nature joy cannot be destroyed. It is the indelible mark of life that lives freely out of its Creator rather than out of some mythical self-established self.

===

EXERCISE 27: JOY

This exercise can help your realization of God's joy in you, and of your joy in God and creation.

1. Try to relax whatever your body and mind may be holding onto. Let these be replaced by a sense of simple trust in God.

2. You may want to read a brief scriptural passage, such as the one cited from John 15:11, or Psalm 18:19, NAB: "God brought me forth into an open place; he delivered me, because he delighted in me."

3. Pray for your openness to embody God's joy in your creation, and your joy in God. See if you can be in touch with God's yearning for the fullness of your joy, and your yearning for God's fullness in you and creation.

4. Invite that joy through your breath for the next ten minutes or longer. As you very slowly breathe in, let your intent be to breathe in God's joy in creating you, a joy that fills every dimension of your being. As you breathe out, let your intent be to breathe out your joy in God. Breathe out with a monotoned sound, "ahhhhhh," like a long sigh.

5. Now broaden your horizon. As you breathe in, let your intent be to breathe in God's joy in all of creation. When you breathe out (still accompanied by "ahhhhhh"), let your intent be to breathe out your joy in God's creation. Do this for another ten minutes or so.

You need not have any particular images or thoughts as you do steps 4 and 5. It is your simple intent that counts. Give God room to empower the joy as God wills. You may come to a point where you even lose your particular intent in breathing in and out and there is nothing left but your naked intent of presence to God, and perhaps a gifted quality of pervasive joy beyond subject and object.

Even if you have no personal sense of joy at this time, you can at least be willing to listen for God's joy. The full realization of this joy is a gift which we cannot force, but which we can invite and be thankful for when it comes.

REFLECTION QUESTIONS

1. What did this prayer show you about joy, and its distinction from, and relation to, pleasure?
2. What past experiences of this kind of joy can you recall in your life?
3. Are there any particular barriers to your reception of joy (for example, a sense that you do not "deserve" it)?
4. Are there other ways you might invite your awareness of joy (for example, reading Scripture with the intent of touching God's joy in us through the words)?

TRUSTING THE PROMISE

Amidst all the seeming ups and downs of our personal lives, and of life in the world, we need to remain appreciative of God's hope in us and promise for creation, so powerfully revealed in Christ. Scripture, tradition, and the Spirit of Christ's direct presence in our hearts, forms in us an obscure vision of paradise. Its full realization is our deepest desire. Our possessive little selves cannot inherit this paradise, and all their attempts to build their own version are at best dim, distorted, or unfulfilling imitations of what the Spirit alone can inspire. So we must learn to listen to the Spirit alive in our midst, and not confuse it with our little self's desire for aggrandizement. We need to trust that the Spirit has in mind for us more than we can imagine (Eph. 3:20), which frees us to approach the guiding Truth with a truly open heart.

In following the Spirit's lead as best we can, we will cooperate with God's mysterious evolution of a fully reconciled and joyful creation. Our personal and social visions and actions will be soaked with what the Spirit forms in us, always beyond our full comprehension. With childlike hearts, yet vigilant minds, we will ever more fully take our unique place in the wonder of creation, trusting that, in the end, all things will be well. "Every kind of thing will be well."[6]

Part 2

SUPPORTING:
PRACTICING THE PRESENCE
IN SMALL GROUPS

Forming the spiritual heart is intrinsically a communal process in Christian tradition. God's very nature is seen as ultimate Loving Community; our human nature reflects that image.

The Holy Spirit circulates gifts among us in countless ways; *between* us we are formed. The "us" is very big. The Spirit blows where it will. On one level, then, spiritual community is where we find it: in chance encounters, in our time with family, friends, coworkers, and oppressed people, through reading, film, and the arts. On a more intentional level, though we find spiritual community with others who care in an ongoing way about their deepening conversion. "Where two or three are gathered together in my name, there I am in the midst of them" (Matt. 18:20). This happens whenever people gather in response to the stirring of their spiritual heart and its call to further unfolding of their distinctive yet shared Christ-nature. Formally we see this gathering in corporate liturgies. Informally we see it in numerous kinds of gatherings for prayer, study, discernment, service, witness, and fellowship.

I would like to describe one intentional small group process that has born much fruit for more than a thousand people over many years now: a long-term group for spiritual formation developed by the Shalem Institute. The introductory group normally meets weekly for four to five months (this can be shortened to as few as six weeks in special situations), with an optional continuing group. The nature of this group was first described in a book by Gerald May, *Pilgrimage Home* in 1979.[1] A chapter on "Group Direction" in my book, *Spiritual Friend*[2] draws out other dimensions of such a group. Our understanding has continued to evolve since then, along with our sense of its adaptability for groups in churches, seminaries, and other settings. All the "lenses" for attending life in the Spirit described in the chapters of part 1 of this book can form the content for such a group.

CHAPTER 9

Intent and Method

What I say in this and the next two chapters is meant to help those who might want to form and lead a long-term group for spiritual formation, in the light of the Shalem Institute's experience. If you are reading this book primarily for your own development apart from group leadership, you may want to skip this part. However, you might find much of part 2 at least indirectly, and often directly, helpful to your personal spiritual understanding and practice.

The particular kind of group described is only one kind of spiritual formation gathering. Others may more directly emphasize such things as study, social concerns, liturgy, healing, charismatic experience, personal witness, or art forms. The Shalem-type group may overlap in its content with many of the above, but its steady intent is cultivation of our direct presence to God as found in contemplative tradition.

WHY THIS KIND OF GROUP?

We can respond to the invitation to join a spiritual formation group for all kinds of reasons, some of them not very conscious or clear. These may have little or nothing to do with the purpose of this kind of group. We might come to support someone else present, a spouse or friend. We might respond out of guilt from the pressure of someone trying to recruit us. Or we may want to come for psychological support, or to talk about books and ideas. If we have a strong but insecure faith, we may come to defend and reinforce what we believe rather than be open for anything new to which God may be inviting us.

Or we may more authentically respond out of that sense of "something deep inside is moving" that I described at the beginning of chapter 1, something that we vaguely sense is more than psychological rumblings. We may have a clear sense of being called to deeper communion by God, or we may have only a vague sense of yearning and search. In either case we feel the need for an environment that can help us face into this mysterious depth of our lives in a disciplined way with others over a period of time.

Behind this desire may lie a sense that without such a group we will be more likely to evade or lose what is occurring inside. Part of us is frightened by this deep stirring and just wants it to go away. Our egos sense a threat to their seeming control and autonomy. We fear disorientation and not knowing what may come of all this. A group and its leader might give us the courage and security to better trust what is happening.

Another motivation might be a sense of not knowing how to attend this mysterious Presence very well. We want to learn some deeper ways of praying, and we want to learn with others whose collective energy, motivation, and experience can strengthen and give perspective to our own.

When we come primarily out of such positive motivations, the group can be a spiritual powerhouse. Everyone shares a certain vulnerability to the Spirit at work in them. We bring a certain willingness beyond all the resistance to attend our deepest emerging self in God, and to be supportive of others doing the same. The seventeenth-century Quaker Isaac Penington vividly describes such a gathering in his day: "They are like a heap of fresh and living coals, warming one another as a great strength, freshness, and vigor of life flows into all."[3]

In my experience with Shalem groups, I do not believe that the particular people who come together for a long-term group are present by accident. Most of them seem to have an incredible readiness to be with this group of people at this particular time, even though they usually do not know one another beforehand. This "right fit" is shown not only by the remarkable spiritual opening that is seen individually, but in the many ways other individuals in the group serve this opening. It is a mini-experience of the Body of Christ, with an amazing complementarity of parts through which the Spirit moves, upbuilding the Body. This process is aided by an atmosphere in which people are helped to drop behind the normal ego surface to that more open place where we become alert to God at work and more simple and clear channels of the Spirit.

The underlying intent of this particular kind of spiritual formation group is to provide prayerful environments that assist a more subtle and pervasive noticing of Christ's Spirit at work in and among us, and of our resistances to it, along with a gradually more willing turn to that Spirit as the heart of our deepest identity.

One-to-one spiritual direction (spiritual friendship with one other person over time) shares this intent as well. In this sense the group includes a form of spiritual direction, that is, of a relationship aimed at assisting our noticing of the direction of the Spirit in our lives, and our positive and negative responses to it. The group adds, as we shall see, dimensions of more frequent meeting, more people sharing together, more guided and silent experiential means of presence to God, and usually more of a teaching and learning dimension.

The formation group is not necessarily a substitute for one-to-one spiritual direction (or its equivalent in small groups organized exclusively for spiritual direction). Some people are involved with both at the same time. One-to-one or group spiritual direction normally provides far more time to reflect in depth together on the particular movements of the Spirit in our life, time which is especially important when we are facing major external vocational discernment or internal discernment of significant spiritual movements. Spiritual direction also normally provides clearer personal accountability for one's uniquely evolving spiritual life over the long haul.

METHOD

In spiritual formation it is vital to keep intent and method closely connected. If our intent is to form the spiritual eye that can notice the Divine Spirit at work, and the spiritual heart that can respond, then everything a group does needs to be guided by this intent. If the leader and group members are not fully committed to this purpose, then the group can easily be taken over by other intents. This may be very subtle. The methods and words may still sound like the above intent is there, but beneath the surface other intents have taken over. I described some of these diversionary intents at the beginning of chapter one. Others might include a desire for socializing, feeling good, or cognitive insights. I will say a little about each of these.

Socializing. The intent to socialize is present when we come to the group out of loneliness or just wanting to be with other people, but not particularly caring about a deeper relationship with God. This can lead to a certain tepid and casual spiritual presence that deflates the group's seriousness.

Feeling good. We live in a society that puts great weight on emotional "highs." It is very tempting to come to a group out of personal and spiritual boredom hoping for some new adrenalin rush, that is made more exciting because we can associate it with God. St. Francis de Sales would have said that this is "wanting the honey without the bread." The honey represents the gifts of God. The bread represents our direct relation to the Giver of the gifts. The honey is a by-product of a deeper intrinsic relationship. The group is designed to attend that relationship, not to stoke up emotions.

This is not to say that many emotions may rightly be evoked as a by-product of attending that relationship. All our emotions will come into play over time as we are cleansed, confronted, illuminated, and loved into deeper spiritual awareness. Our proper intent, though, will keep us focused on our direct relationship with God, and not let us become too fascinated with the emotional fallout itself. Such undue attention to the emotional fireworks not only deflects the person involved away from God, but it can deflect others as well. They may become caught up in the person's enthusiastic descriptions of powerful experiences and feel badly that they have no equivalent experience, thinking that this is what it's all about. In fact, the seeming "nonexperience" of such people, the "plainness" of their awareness, may point to the real divine relationship that is present. This relationship does not depend on any particular feeling tone. It is beyond our feelings. Because of this, though, it can seem nonexistent if we are looking for immediate emotional evidence. Our deepest relationship with God is so plain that we can easily miss it if we don't attend it in the plainness, the simple spaciousness, of our awareness.

Insights. We might come to the group primarily to develop new mental images and ideas about God. This is a worthy motive on one level. Conceptual and imaginal insight into our spiritual nature can help bridge us into our direct relationship with God. When we include the mental images and ideas of Scripture and tradition as well as our own, then we also have some guidelines for testing and guiding our understanding and way of approaching God, creation, and self. The temptation, though, is to make the bridge the goal: we take our conceptual understanding and images as the ultimate reality for us. We are satisfied with what we can grasp. But what we can conceptually grasp is not the primary goal of such a spiritual formation group.

The goal once again is attending our direct relationship with God, and this is beneath and beyond our conceptual grasp. Our insights can point us toward that relationship, but the relationship itself is more direct, intimate, immediate, free, and intrinsic to our nature than the insights themselves. Like feelings, insights can indicate the reality of the relationship, but the relationship itself precedes the indicators, and is more stable and pervasive.

All of us will enter such a spiritual formation group with a certain fear as well as yearning for attending this direct relationship. The stronger the yearning and empowering grace at hand (that is, God's sense of our readiness), the more likely we will be able to let the many diverting intentions I have mentioned remain on the fringe. The stronger the fear we bring, the more easily we will be tempted to be diverted. Behind such fear is our difficulty in trusting God so nakedly, without holding on to our many "props" that keep our egos feeling more in control and "self" possessed.

We can also be diverted by confusion about what in the world a direct relationship with God really is. Most of us have had little conditioning for understanding or cultivating such a relationship. Our religious culture tends to stop at the level of concept, image, feeling, and moral action. Cultivating the direct awareness that grounds all of these in God moment by moment is advocated in Scripture (e.g., John 14–17 and Paul's prayer in Eph. 3), but without much methodological guideline. We are given more precise help in the writings we have inherited from later contemplative tradition. However, contemplative spiritual formation is centrally an *oral* tradition (as Christ taught his disciples), and most of us have not had opportunity to be with people who have long-term, careful formation in contemplative awareness. Because of this, the need for evolving the kind of spiritual formation group and leadership described here is very great.

Such a group can be a precious opportunity for people. However, because of our fear and confusion, the life of any group inevitably is going to be marked by a melange of graced moments, diverted times, and what seems like much fumbling around in the dark. What most counts is that we pay highest attention to our yearning for God and God's yearning for us through all of the ins and outs, and that we steadily pray for that graced trust that frees us to relinquish ourselves to God, believing that all we have to lose is our chains. Steady prayer for this trust is vital, because we are very tempted to prefer a chain we know to the freedom and callings of God that we do not yet know.

From all I have said so far it should be clear that what is most crucial in a spiritual formation group is paying attention to our intent through whatever technical methods for praying and meditation we bring to bear. One more part of our conditioning reinforces this need even more, that is, our societal tendency to become fascinated with technology in every field of life. In such a cultural climate particular methods can easily become ends in themselves. We are tempted to use them without regard for the ways they serve or divert our primary purpose. They can become accumulated bits and pieces of unrelated spiritual technology that have their own way of becoming fetishes. Then the methods divert us from God and our deeper self in God, ironically in the name of God.

Yet we cannot escape the need for particular methods, that is, particular ways through which we can pay attention to God. Methods are good as long as we remember that they are means and not ends, bridges and not the shore. Certain methods are described in part 1 of this book in relation to various "lenses" of life through which we approach God. No group need include all the lenses nor all the suggested methods related to them. It is easier to cut down on the quantity of methods introduced in a group if we remember that each method is a window into the same reality of God and human spirit. The more experience we have in prayer and meditation, the more we realize that we are not dealing with different categories of reality when we pray through Scripture, an icon, confession, singing, vocational discernment, and so on. We are simply shifting the camera lens of our spiritual eye to different focal settings, each of which has its own potential way of being used by God to bring us nearer to our awareness of divine presence.

However, the particular method called for at a given time will vary from person to person. If people in a group do not have much experience with different kinds of prayer and meditation methods, they can benefit from the opportunity of being exposed to a basic range of forms in order to find the one or two that most assist their presence to God. Once discovered, these can be taken on as part of a long-term daily practice. If participants are encouraged to take any particularly promising method offered in a weekly group and practice it on a daily basis between meetings as a means of attentiveness to God, they will have more time to test out its value for them. Regardless of the methods used, all participants should be encouraged and committed to spend at least half an hour a day (preferably twice a day) in unambiguous prayer, including time for just silently "being there," directly present to God.

Participants may already have their own appropriate pattern for this daily time and what is done together in the group need not enter that daily practice. However, members need to be sensitive during the week to what was done in the group as a possible window to God for them. This might be noticed at any time during the day, not just during special personal prayer time. The special group time, after all, is basically an intensive period of sharpening our spiritual eye so that we can more readily notice and respond to the grace at hand all the time.

The range of methods introduced in a group will depend on the experience of the leader(s). Shalem introductory groups normally include methods representing most of the lenses for attending God that are presented in the chapters of part 1. Such a broad range is neither necessary nor possible in shorter groups, however. Often it is good to repeat a method, or some variation of it, for two or three weeks running or longer. This gives people more time to move beyond the mechanics of the method and let it become a little simpler means of presence to God.

It is worth considering the possibility of relating the exercise to any major seasons of the Church Year that may occur during the course of the group, especially if many members come from a tradition that emphasizes these. Such tie-ins can help bridge people's experience into the larger Church's ongoing remembrance of God's varied forms of presence for us. This can happen simply by making some verbal connections to Christmas, Epiphany, Lent, Easter, Pentecost, etc., or else the method itself may be selected in relation to the season. This might mean, for example, selecting a seasonally relevant scriptural text for prayer, or a visualization of light during Epiphany, or a focus on bodily and mental fasting during Lent. However, the internal integrity of the flow of methods used needs to take priority over liturgical seasons.

What counts most is a flow that will be most helpful to the evolving interior presence for God of group members.

Some people in a group may already have experience with one or more of the methods introduced. Their experience can help them more easily drop to a simple recollected presence. Their past experience can be helpful to others, as well. Therefore it is not necessary to try and provide totally new methods for everyone in the group.

In *sequencing* particular methods, it is probably best to begin with one that at least overlaps with something familiar to participants, such as scriptural prayer. This will help bridge to their past experience and give them a little more initial security in the group. In intentional spiritual formation everyone needs enough security to prevent unnecessary anxiety from rising and becoming an obstacle to prayerful presence. On the other hand, oversecuring a group can lead to complacency and hinder the challenging edge of God's presence from showing itself. Spiritual formation includes an ongoing purging of idols, attachments, and pretense. These fall away as we are graced and willing. The attitude called for toward oneself in a group thus involves trust in God's active grace, that is God's liberating presence for us. It also calls for trust in God's timing (rather than our own) for our awareness of that grace. We need to *accept* ourselves fully where and as we are, yet not have to *affirm* ourself in a defensive way that blunts our growing edge.

CHAPTER 10

Rhythm

The particular flow of group time is important. If participants can predict a fairly regular pattern in the progress of a two-hour session, it frees them to worry less about the externals and to sink more easily into God's presence through whatever content is introduced. The rhythm that we have honed over the years is marked by the following seven periods (normally, but not necessarily, in this order):

1. Gathering in silence
2. Beginning together
3. Body prayer
4. Guidance into attentive silence
5. Journal keeping and rest
6. Sharing
7. Closure

1. GATHERING IN SILENCE.

Gathering in silence sets the tone for a different kind of mutual presence than is usual for people. Rather than falling into normal habits of social exchange with each other, we fall into the spaciousness of collective silence.

Normally we gather in a circle (sitting either in chairs or on cushions or prayer benches), with a candle in the middle. The circle can symbolize the wholeness of life that exists in God, illuminated for us by the light of Christ in our midst. More practically, the circle gives everyone a front row seat, expressing our equality before God and our need for attention to our firsthand relationship with God. Finally, silence in a circle can help to empower our meshing of both communal and solitary dimensions of our spiritual being. We are part of an interdependent Body on a corporate journey here, with a shared intent, support, and capacity to reverberate Christ's liberating Spirit among us. At the same time the silence gives us a spacious solitude together. The mind is freed to begin a process of recollection, dropping through the fragmented surface toward a more integral presence to God, and to the world in God.

A very interesting recent research study[1] sought answers to the question: "Have you ever felt that you were very close to a powerful spiritual force that seemed to lift you out of yourself?" The majority of respondents said that such experiences occurred when they were *alone*. Perhaps this relates to Jesus' injunction, "When you pray, go into your room, and shut the door. . . ." (Matt. 6:6). Yet Jesus also speaks of being present where two or three are gathered in his name. These apparent differences find common ground in a contemplative spiritual formation group. We are together, but with a quality of communal solitude. One of the great problems of community without such solitude is that as the above research study concludes, we are then under pressure to conform to the expectations of others, and to fit in with the accepted and approved knowledge system of our society. The kind of contemplative group I am describing can cultivate freedom from this pressure, without losing the strength and awareness of spiritual community.

Cultivation of this way of being with others can bear much fruit beyond the group time. It can encourage more free and deep prayer alone that drops to the common ground of self, neighbor, and God. It also can condition a way of being in work, family, friendship, liturgy, and other layers of community with an inner spiritual gyroscope that frees us from dulling cultural conformity, and for authentic discernment and action.

2. BEGINNING TOGETHER.

When the group has formed, the leader gathers everyone's attention by gently ringing a bell or clapping hands. Then everyone brings their hands together in a prayerful gesture and together we bow in physical recognition of God's presence in and among us. As we bow we chant the single Hebrew word, "shalom." Practically, that shared sound draws us together as one body. Symbolically, it expresses and reinforces our desire for God's fullness, for the just peace that passes understanding, which the biblical word *shalom* connotes.

This particular way of beginning is not essential, but some way of ritually and regularly beginning together can be helpful in setting the corporate tone for the gathering.

3. BODY PRAYER.

The group is now offered some means for sharpening direct awareness of God and softening resistance and distraction. Normally this begins with attention to the body for about fifteen minutes. "Embodiment" in spiritual formation is the subject of chapter 2, so I will be very brief in what I say here. People usually come to groups with tense and often tired bodies. Given the close connection between mind and body, a little attention to assisting the body's relaxed, open alertness can do wonders for our presence to God. Sometimes just a few long, slow, deep breaths together can be enough. If you are introducing a number of exercises for the body during the course of a group, it is better to repeat a few basic, simple ones rather than introduce the distracting potential of too many or too complex ones. Also, it is good to introduce exercises that can be a form of "body prayer" rather than just preliminaries to prayer. Finally, it is ideal when the exercises can be related to the particular method of prayer that follows them, though this is not essential.

4. GUIDANCE INTO ATTENTIVE SILENCE.

Normally the prayer method used here is introduced with a few minutes of background that gives a helpful context for its understanding and practice. The method also can be briefly related to whatever prayer method preceded it. Such bridging can help save it from being seen as a totally new, unconnected practice, rather than simply as another "way in" to the same reality of God. Such a sense of continuity can help our minds to remain "even" through all methods used, rather than becoming distracted or fragmented by the surface differences, or caught up in learning methods as ends in themselves.

The introduction needs to be aimed at preparing people to be drawn into an awareness, or at least trust, of God's presence with the help of the method. Anything that distracts from this preparation needs to be left aside. For example, if Centering Prayer is being introduced (exercise 5), there are many interesting things that could be said about its history, its relationship to other forms of prayer, its difficulties, and so on. But if the result is to draw people into a thick jungle of mental association and whet their curiosity to ask questions, then the intent of preparation for prayer has been subverted. The introduction should give people just enough understanding to ease their way into the practice, along with a clear, simple description of the practice. No discussion whatsoever should take place until after the practice. This would only detract from the quality of interior recollection that hopefully is beginning to evolve now. This recollection is very delicate and easily lost, especially for beginners. The group is providing a precious opportunity for support of this still, open presence. There will be time afterward for more detailed descriptions and questioning if this is called for. These will be understood better, in any case, once the group has had a firsthand experience with the method.

Most methods will lead the group into a collective silence. This silence may last as little as ten minutes early in a group's life, and slowly expand to half an hour or longer as the group progresses. The leader can bring the group out of the silence with a bell, clapped hands, or a word.

5. JOURNAL KEEPING AND REST.

The group is given about ten minutes in silence for any kind of written reflection on the time in silence. For those who are not drawn to writing, it is a time for relaxation, which for some may include lying down (which is one good reason to be in a carpeted room).

As the weeks go on, the leader can occasionally ask people to notice the same even background mind through these various shifts in activity during the evening. Such a reminder can help people to counter the cultural conditioning that leads us to jerk our minds from one seemingly discrete category of presence to another in a way that fragments our consciousness and buries our recollection.

6. SHARING.

Something in us often yearns to share what is happening in our prayer and probing with the deep Wellspring of our lives, especially in its early stages. Expression on paper sometimes feels sufficient. At times we will feel like sharing with other people, too. Our minds want to say something about the often vague yet palpably real stirrings and stillness of our heart. On the positive side, such sharing with others can help our minds to claim what our hearts vaguely know. We learn to communicate with ourselves and others something of our spiritual awareness and responsiveness. We make mental connections between these and the rest of our lived experience. We probe the implications of the interior awareness for our way of understanding and living out our life.

In listening to others share, we become more aware of the marvelous wealth of experience between us. We hear the Spirit's footsteps in others and we are encouraged; our sense of possibilities is broadened, and we are made aware of the larger Body of grace we share. We also are consoled when we find that we are not alone in our distractions and sense of struggle.

On the negative side, this kind of sharing raises certain dangers earlier mentioned. We might become competitive with others' experiences, feel like failures if nothing comparable seems to be happening with us, and mistake the experiences as ultimate rather than penultimate. Then we are tempted to grasp after experiences of God rather than relaxing directly into God. At bottom this direct presence seems to be marked normally not by fireworks but by a plain, spacious awareness that is so simple we might easily feel that nothing at all is happening.

Another potential problem with sharing is that we might place too much weight on rational mental clarity, as though such attempts at articulation are closer to what is real than the more vague sense of presence when we are not trying to grasp it with our minds. As we explored more fully in the chapter on "Seeing," once we begin thinking "about" what is happening, we have stepped outside of it and split ourselves away, in order to make operational our cognitive capacity to describe and interpret, that is, to bring mental clarity.

The cognitive mind has its rightful spiritual place as communicator, connector, integrator, and critic. But it cannot finally "grasp" the mystery of God and our deepest identity. These finally must be lived and obscurely noticed from the "inside." As this realization evolves over months and years of spiritual attention, we begin to notice that cognitive articulation becomes more optional and relativized to a simple precognitive awareness that is present and sufficient, without need for great struggles to understand and categorize (though some kinds of personalities will continue to be more steadily attracted to such struggle than others). This awareness lies behind those repeated classical descriptions of "how it is" in mature times of the spiritual life, descriptions that one way or another point to a great simplicity, ordinariness, and immediate, trusting presence in our interior and daily living.

Most people who join a group for spiritual formation are not likely to be at this point most of the time. But it is important to be sensitive to this possibility and give people permission to remain silent in a group. Sometimes people just need to sit with their experience and trust God to continue working secretly in their silent, open mind without need of their thinking about or sharing what is happening. For them this might dissipate their evolving spiritual awareness rather than reinforce it. Silent people then need not be seen as only introverted or unconfident people, afraid to share, who need to be drawn out (though this may account for some people's silence). People's silence sometimes just needs to be trusted as right for them at a particular time.

For those who need to share, however, groups need to be small enough for everyone to be able to say what they need to. If a group has more than seven or eight people, I think it is good to divide them into subgroups of three to six people, depending on how much time is available (the smaller the time, the smaller the group). Shalem's long-term introductory groups normally are divided into sub-groups of four. Sometimes these are predetermined by the leader and become permanent arrangements for the duration of the group. If this is done, some care needs to be taken to put people together who will likely be right for each other, yet keeping the group diverse enough to provide broad perspective. Mixing men and women together, for example, is one of our regular guidelines. Factors of age, personality, and spiritual background also need to be attended in arranging such groups.

One alternative to prearranged groups is to have changing groups each week that are made by counting off or by some other method. If the overall size of the group is small, say a dozen or less, this will likely work better than in larger groups, because the participants will probably have some sense of each other through plenary sharing times. In larger groups, though, the great disadvantage of changing subgroups is that people do not have an opportunity to build rapport and security with one another that can free them to share more easily.[2]

Another alternative is to subdivide into permanent or changing pairs. This can be valuable in certain situations, but it has some disadvantages: the group may not be even numbered; the personalities may grate on one another; if one person feels called to silence, it is much more difficult for them to remain so; and if the pairs are permanent, people will be left alone whenever their partners are absent (unless more than one person is absent and the remaining partners are paired).

Shalem introductory groups normally provide about twenty-five minutes for sharing in small groups. How can this time be spent in a way that keeps people close to that direct presence to God for which the whole group exists? The most important guideline for this is advocacy of a prayerful presence to each other. This is not a time for psychological or theological analysis. The intent is much simpler: to describe our quality of presence to God and our sense of God's presence to us during the silence, and if relevant, during the past week. When we have finished, the group can surround our words with a supportive and prayerful silence. No one need respond orally. No one needs to feel pressure to be "helpful." Our silent presence is support enough. Let the silence turn the words toward God.

Once in a while a member of the group may be moved to ask a simple question to draw out more clarity or some implications for another person of what was said, but this is not essential. A special kind of intimacy and penetration can result from such a way of being together. It involves a certain austerity of words, to insure that everyone remains present to the spacious Ground out of which they rise.

The group leader can sometimes assist the focus of these sharing groups by suggesting one or two questions to be used for several minutes of personal reflection (mental or written) before corporate sharing. These questions would be aimed at drawing out certain dimensions of awareness. Examples of such questions follow the description of most exercises in this book. Besides such questions you might ask: What one word describes the quality of your awareness now? Did you notice a connection between this way of being present to God and the method we used last week? Again, we would hope for more penetration than elaboration in answering these questions: a simple description of the experience and awareness, and perhaps a simple connection with other experiences in one's life.

In difficult subgroup situations there is need for some kind of monitoring, that is, some way to gently call the group back to its purpose if this is being undermined, or to remind people of the need to give one another equal time for sharing if everyone is wanting to say something and someone is inappropriately dominating. Often group members are aware of the need for such monitoring, but they sometimes feel reluctant to say anything without a specifically designated role for this, even if the leader has suggested such monitoring as a shared role. If there is no such reluctance, then group members can monitor one another informally without the need for a designated person. This is the way Shalem subgroups function. It is preferable in freeing everyone to be openly present. In unusually difficult situations the leader might sit in with the group occasionally and try to model such monitoring.

Moving away from the divine fire in the group is to be expected at times. Something in us wants to escape into more domestic conversation. We all know the contradictory interior tugs toward and away from God. The group can become mutual conspirators in evasion of God, or mutual supporters in facing into God's fiery love, trusting more than fearing its slowly transforming heat (which may be felt or may be more secretly at work in us). Every group needs to pray for a trusting facing-in to God's presence.

When group members have much experience with collective silence, one alternative way of sharing is more strictly prayerful and sparse. This way would find its closest parallel in a silent Quaker Meeting. It can happen with a large group or small one. Everyone begins in silence together. No one speaks unless moved from the spiritual heart to share something. This sharing usually is very brief and pithy. It involves a less consciously reflective, more simple and direct awareness. The shared intention is for a deep listening to God together, and a willingness to be a spontaneous channel of grace for others and receptor of grace through others.

No one knows ahead of time whether they will have anything to share. There is less sense of personal possession of anything said. Something rises and comes through us with great simplicity. It may be a phrase of Scripture; it may be a sense of who God or we are, or what we are called to do, incubated out of one's prayer that session and brought to light in this moment. What comes may be something that proves to be of value to others in the group as well as for oneself, as we circulate the Spirit's Word erupting among us. Sometimes nothing is said out loud, and the collective silence alone is the gift. The value of this means of mutual presence extends beyond the time together, as it conditions us for listening and sharing in every form of community more deeply and simply.

When this form of sharing is done, it is usually best to let it be the sufficient form of sharing for the session. Moving into a more analytical plenary time about the session's experience can unnecessarily dissipate the centered presence that normally will be there for most people. However, if the more reflective small group sharing described earlier takes place, then such a plenary session can prove valuable for many participants. This is a time when the leader might have a general question or two for group members about their awareness, or about some confusion related to the method used that session. Members of the group may have their own questions to ask here, or perhaps a deep shared insight has emerged in a subgroup that could be valuable for all to hear (this may have a humorous edge at times, which can be good when the atmosphere has become over intense and grasping).

Such a plenary time normally would last from about ten to no more than thirty minutes. It gives the whole group a chance to be "felt whole" again, with an open-ended opportunity for reflection. However, if the group is large, more extroverted people will tend to dominate. One way of mitigating this tendency is for the leader to suggest a standard that no one speak more than once unless no one else has anything to say.

Toward the end of the plenary session the leader might suggest some experiential homework for daily practice during the week ahead. This normally would relate to the method of prayer used that evening. The leader also might suggest a particular Scriptural phrase for attention during the week that relates to the method. For example, if the method involves a visualization of healing, cleansing light, the scriptural phrase might be Christ's proclamation, "I am the light of the world" (John 8:12). People should be asked not to analyze such a phrase too much, but rather just to let it live beneath their conscious mind and ask for the grace of that phrase for them to be revealed during the week. After introducing the phrase, the leader can ask the group to slowly repeat it to themselves for a moment in silence, perhaps in rhythm with their breathing, letting it gently sink beneath the surface of the mind.

Some people might use the phrase as a constantly repeated prayer during the week, letting it draw them to God's presence in the midst of various circumstances of the day. Sometimes it spontaneously simplifies itself to one or two words. In the following week's session, the leader might ask the group to share any particularly graced or difficult experience with the phrase during subgroup time.

7. CLOSURE.

During the last three to five minutes of group time it is good to have a clear way of ending together. Over the years Shalem groups have done this by having several minutes of silence for the offering of any intercessions people may have for the world (sometimes joining hands during this time). This provides a helpful transition to the larger world, leaving people with a sense of prayerful concern not only for themselves but for the stewardship of the earth and its life together in God. The group's circle is extended, in effect, to include God's whole circle of creation. Some groups include praying orally for the person next to them in the circle by name (in the form of intercession or thanksgiving), expressing in effect the group's prayer for that person. That prayer hopefully is continued through the week. This practice seems particularly meaningful when the group comes from the same church. It also can be particularly valuable for people who have never been personally prayed for before, opening them to God's love through another person in this way.

Our last act together in a Shalem group is the same one with which we began: our hands are brought together in front of us, and a common bow is made along with a chanted "shalom." Informal conversation is allowed following the meeting, in contrast to the way we gathered in silence. Some people leave immediately, others may linger a few minutes to share further with one another or the leader.

LONGER FIRST AND LAST DAYS

Shalem's experience in launching a long-term group points to the value of beginning with a longer than usual session. When the group gathers together on the first day, its members bring many hidden questions. Who are all these people? Can I really let myself be vulnerable to God with them? I've never been through something like this before. What's going to happen? Can I trust the leader?

Such questions as these rise naturally at the start of a spiritual formation group of this nature. The first meeting together is particularly important for developing an atmosphere where everyone feels personally in touch with their own spiritual condition, and in touch with the members and nature of the group. With this foundation people can be present in future sessions with a little less anxiety and a little more freedom to relax into the process of the group, and hopefully to relax more with God and one another.

We normally begin a group with a session that lasts for about six hours. The time can be structured in many good ways. The First Day Session outline shows one way of doing it. The time might be morning and afternoon or afternoon and evening, on a weekday or a weekend, depending on group members' schedules. I have arbitrarily chosen a morning and afternoon for the sake of this outline.

FIRST DAY SESSION

10:00 A.M. Gathering time, with casual conversation. This is the one time the group does not gather in silence. It is helpful to provide name tags, and coffee and tea.

10:15 Form a circle. Begin with about five minutes of relaxing long breaths and silence. Ask the group members to be in touch with their own hope in being here, and to shape that hope into a silent prayer.

10:20 Ask everyone to introduce themselves, spending one to five minutes (depending on the size of the group) saying a little about who they are and what brings them to this group.

10:45 The leader provides (1) a brief outline of the day's intent and schedule, (2) a brief word about the nature of journal keeping, perhaps mentioning that journals will be the main "text" for the group, since they symbolize our intent of drawing out our firsthand experience with God, surrounded by Scripture, the group, and other resources, and (3) *optionally,* a brief bibliographical handout for recommended current and historical spiritual reading besides Scripture. We do not usually require any particular reading, but some groups may find such a shared background helpful. The important thing is not to allow reading to take the place of attention to our firsthand evolving spiritual awareness. To reinforce this, the leader may prefer to delay handing out a bibliography until later or at the end of the group, or not at all.

If subgroups are to be included in the group's life, the leader provides a handout of subgroup members, usually four or five to a group, preselected by the leader if appropriate (see previous discussion of small groups), along with a brief and clear word about the intent of these groups.

The leader should also give a word about their own role in the group (see chapter 11 about this).

11:15 Brief break, either open or in the form of a few simple corporate relaxation exercises.

11:25 Instructions for some way of getting in touch with one's spiritual journey, ideally some way that brings both intuitive and analytical faculties to bear. This personal reflection time would last about forty-five minutes. The particular means might include some kind of open-ended drawing on a blank piece of paper made with a choice of crayons, to bring out an intuitive awareness, e.g., "Draw a picture of reality as you experience it, moving into this with an open, relaxed mind." A person might want to add a few descriptive words afterward, perhaps a series of free-association phrases, or a poem. This could be followed by asking people to outline some of the major "footsteps of God" in their life, going back to childhood if they like. This in turn could be followed by a handout with three simple questions. My spiritual journey: (1) What does it seem to be? (2) How does it seem to happen? (3) What do I seem to need now?[3]

12:10 p.m. Ask them to gather in their subgroups and share with one another whatever they feel comfortable in sharing.

(11:30–12:55) During this period, while the group is occupied as just described, the leader might want to call out individual members of the group and spend five to ten minutes meeting privately with them in a separate room, especially if they are strangers. If the group is too large to meet with everyone alone in the time allotted, then the leader can meet with two people at a time (if there are two leaders, the group can be divided between them). The leader's questions could be aimed at drawing out their particular hopes and anxieties in being here, perhaps ending with a prayer for them. Such a meeting could instead precede this first day either in person or by phone. In this case it can include questions that probe the rightness or wrongness of this kind of group for them at this time in their lives. These few minutes either before or during the opening day can help sensitize the leader to the situation of particular people, affecting what he or she says and hears in the course of the group. It also can aid a spiritual bonding with them.

12:55 Collect the written and drawn materials, if people are willing to let them go. Reading them over after the group can further sensitize the leader to the spiritual situation of members. They can be handed back during the last session to help people notice the difference and similarity of their spiritual awareness between the beginning and end of the group's life. Participants should be assured of the confidentiality of this work.

1:00 Lunch. The group can be asked ahead of time to bring something to share. This can aid its communal spirit.

2:00 The leader introduces the group's intents and process. An outline of methods and dates of use might be given out here, but this is not essential and might even deflect people away from the sacred intent of relinquishing to God through all methods, putting too much weight on anticipation of the methods themselves. It also can set up expectations that make it more difficult for the leader to make changes as these may be called for in the unpredictable evolution of the group's experience.

Next, the leader might say something about the value of mutual prayer. If there are ongoing subgroups, prayer during the week for fellow members could be particularly encouraged. If there are no subgroups, the leader might divide the group into prayer partners. These pairs could meet occasionally during the group's reflection time (with the risk that some partners might be absent at a given session). Earlier I mentioned the option of mutual intercession during the closing minutes of a regular session. Such mutual prayer becomes a reminder of the communal rather than private context of Christian spiritual life and provides everyone with a sense of someone else in the group who is particularly accountable for holding them up to God.

Such knowledge can have a subtle way of steadying our own personal caring about deepening into God, especially during dry periods.

During this time, the leader might also say something about the potential impact of the group on spouses for those who are married and whose spouse is not in the group. Particular emphasis needs to be given to the realization that spouses rarely are in the same place spiritually, and therefore, differences should be treated with respectful sensitivity. (I have said more about this often neglected subject in chapter 5, "Communing.") What is said of spouses might also be said, with some modifications, for others with whom people may have a close living or working relationship.

Finally, the leader can say something about *group standards*. These can be handed out in written form to give them more weight. The group needs to agree to certain things that will aid the progress and trust level of its members. Standards developed over the years for most Shalem groups fall into two categories.[4] The first involves *relationships within the group.*

1. Silence in the meditation room, except during group reflection and after the session.
2. Giving priority to attendence at group sessions: commitment to coming even when you may not feel like it.
3. Coming to and ending the group on time.
4. No drinking, eating, or smoking in the meditation room itself.
5. Sensitivity to sharing fairly the speaking time in subgroup and plenary reflection periods.
6. Freedom to speak or remain silent in small groups. Accepting one another's experience for what it is without judgment.
7. Letting someone in the group know if you cannot come to a particular meeting, and being responsible for calling a member of the group afterward to find out what happened, including any homework that may have been given.

Hopefully you can support an attitude of attentive patience with yourself, others, the group process, and God, through doubts, frustrations, restlessness, boredom, fear, judgment, grasping, fascination, elation, and so on.

The second list of standards relates to members' *time outside the group meeting:*

1. Daily discipline of attentiveness to God both in solitude and through daily activities. We encourage the goal of a half-hour per day of solitude time. We urge you to explore ways to establish a regular time and place for prayer. This period can include time for both active and quiet prayer, with an emphasis on the latter. Scripture, even if only a single spontaneous phrase that comes to

mind, can be treated as a vital avenue to God's presence during this time.

2. Regular journal keeping (both during the group and outside) to the extent you find this a helpful way of attending God's life in you and the world.

3. Reading anything that may have been assigned for the group.

4. Daily intercessory prayer for the world, including those in your subgroup or your prayer partner.

5. Discrimination in sharing your personal experience in the group with others who are not in it. Indiscriminate sharing may be threatening and difficult for others to understand and also can have a way of replacing the centrality of your interior evolving simple presence.

6. Never sharing what others say about themselves in the group in any personally identifiable way without their permission. This is important for the group's sense of mutual trust that allows one another to share more freely.

2:30 p.m. Introduction to the body's participation in prayer. It is valuable to pay attention to the body early on in the group, since many people have never directly connected it with prayer. Here the leader might demonstrate different possible ways of sitting for prayer and possibly introduce other relevant dimensions of the body, such as gesture, movement, and diet, followed by a guided ten minutes or so experience of slow breathing (see chapter 2, "Embodiment").

3:00 Personal journal reflection on the question: "How do you see and deal with your body in relation to God and prayer?"

3:10 Sharing (in plenary, if it is a small group, otherwise in subgroups) of responses.

3:30 Brief plenary time for questioning or sharing of experience related to the journal reflection question, if subgroups have been used.

3:40 Ask everyone to slowly repeat a particular phrase or verse of Scripture (perhaps in rhythm with their breathing) for about ten minutes, with the intent not of analyzing it but of letting it slowly sink into them as a reminder of God's presence. The Scripture chosen should be simple and accessible to everyone, such as Isaiah 30:15, "In quietness and trust shall be your strength." Afterward, ask the group to continue to be present to God through the chosen verse in the week ahead, letting it rise during the day amidst various activities, as well as in solitude if it seems right. The group might be alerted to the possibility of the verse spontaneously simplifying itself to a few key words.

3:55 Closure. Introduce the chanted "shalom" described earlier, with a brief explanation of its intent and its use at the start and end of each session, followed by a moment of open prayer together, and then actually chanting the "shalom" (see previous discussion of closure in sessions) or otherwise closing the session if the "shalom" is not going to be used in the group.

4:00 End.

LAST DAY SESSION

"What am I going to do after the group ends?" People often are anxious about losing the support of the group. They need time to "look whole" at what has been going on with them during the group's life, to look at their next steps, and to come to closure with the group (or at least with this phase of the group, if it decides to continue). A longer session can be a very helpful time period for accomplishing these ends. Indeed, if time and resources are available, an overnight retreat could be helpful at this point (as well as at the beginning) instead of a longer single day. Such a longer period can be especially helpful in allowing more time for silent meditation periods. But it would be important for everyone to be able to make this commitment.

This time outline shows one, among many possible ways, of structuring a six-hour closing session.

10:00 A.M. Gather in silence.

10:15 Opening "shalom," followed by some physical relaxation exercise and open silence, letting people be present to God through whatever method is most helpful to them at this point.

10:40 Ask everyone to let three words come to mind that describe "spiritual awareness." Go around the group and have each person say their words without any added comments.

10:50 Hand out pieces of blank white paper. Give the same assignment as that given in the first day session. "Draw a picture of reality as you experience it. . . ." This could be followed by participants again answering the three questions posed at the first session. "My spiritual journey: (1) What does it seem to be? (2) How does it seem to happen? (3) What do I seem to need now?"

11:15 Hand back original pictures and answers, collected after the first session. (If some people kept theirs, ask them ahead of time to bring the material with them today.) Ask them to spend several minutes silently comparing the new, and the original material, seeing what the similarities and differences say about their evolving relationship with God and creation, and answering the question, "What kind of support (people, places, times for prayer, etc.) do I need now for further attending God in my life?"

When they are finished ask them to join their long-term subgroups for the last time (if there are none, then share with prayer partners or in plenary). In these groups, ask them to share what feels most important and right to share about their pictures and answers, giving everyone about five minutes or so each. After each person has finished, ask everyone to remain silent for several minutes and reflect on what one thing they want to tell that person about: (1) the grace they sense in that person's life; and (2), what they sense that person needs to attend to in their spiritual life at this point. Suggest spending another five minutes or so for everyone to give their answers to each person, the receiver remaining silent until he or she has heard everyone's comments, then briefly responding in terms of how on target they seemed. Thus a total of at least twelve minutes will have been given for each person (time for their original sharing and for group reflection and response). After everyone has been prayfully attended in this way, join hands in silent and/or open prayer for one another.

12:30 p.m. Potluck lunch.

1:30 Written *evaluation questions* are handed out. These can be designed to be helpful both to participants and leader. For participants, questions can be framed in such a way that they draw out greater clarity concerning where they are and what they need now in their spiritual life. For the sake of the leader, questions can be asked that give feedback about the content, process, and leadership of the group. In long groups a shorter, midterm evaluation with the same dual purpose also can be helpful (along perhaps with a lengthier session that day). Among other benefits, such an evaluation can help the leader be more sensitive to participant struggles, questions, and graces, which can help the leader more appropriately gear what is said and done in the second half of the group. Sample midterm and ending introductory group evaluations can be found in the appendix.

While these evaluations are being filled out the leader can have brief private (or pair) meetings with participants, as on the first day, if the group's size is such that the leader has not been in very personal touch with many of them. A personal question can be asked, such as: "How do you seem to be called now in your prayer life?" Or, "What seems different now in your turning to God?" Answering such questions orally can have a way of reinforcing both clarity and continuing commitment to a deepening spiritual journey. The leader, however, may feel that the earlier dialogue in subgroups or plenary session is sufficient and such a private or semiprivate addition is not called for at this point.

2:30 Plenary session on further resources. "What am I/we called to for further support and challenge?" Now is the time for the leader and others in the group to spell out a range of possibilities that participants may need to bring to prayer, including such things as spiritual direction; a continuing group for a specified amount of time with these or other people; particular personal disciplines; and retreat and study centers. It is important to emphasize the priority resource of God's grace and one's own sincere desire, beyond inevitable resistance, to grow in that grace. This understanding needs to undergird any particular disciplines, which in the end are but ways of inviting, noticing, and sustaining the grace that grows us into our true likeness of God. It is also important to point out the value of cultivating the essential spiritual fruit of love: caring for the world in the particular ways we are called and gifted. (This normally would have been done already in a session on discernment of vocation.)

It might also be helpful at this point, or earlier, to ask people to note just what supports and resists their deepening spiritual life in their particular social world (family, friends, church, work, community). (Such a question might be helpful back on the first day of the group as well.) If the dominant values reflected in these settings are seen to be resistant, this can help people become that much more clear about the importance of intentional ongoing support for their life in God.

If the group has been a particularly graced experience, then there will often be a desire to continue. If this sentiment is expressed, it is important for the leader to test out the subtle difference between a nostalgic desire to hold on to the group simply out of its good memories, versus a positive sense of calling from God to continue together into a new phase. One way of testing this out is for the leader to suggest that everyone pray open-mindedly about their calling for a week or two, and if there is a real sense of desire to let the leader know, and gather back at a specified time. If this happens, a new covenant needs to be made with one another concerning length of commitment, intent, leadership, rhythm, and so forth. Such issues could be listed on a questionnaire, the answers collated by someone, and brought to the group for consensus. It is important for a person to feel free *not* to return just to please the group. The motivation must be from within, or people will not likely stick with it, or not be fully present when they do come.

3:15 Closure with some kind of corporate worship. This is a good time for an informal Eucharist or agape meal together. This can include opportunities for remembering special moments of the group's life, and for open prayer that expresses participants' particular hopes for themselves and the world in God's grace. It also might include a symbolic token gift for everyone, either given by the leader or brought by participants to share. These might include such things as a seed, flower, religious card, poem, or scriptural verse. If "shalom" or some other opening and closing chant has been used in the group, this could be done together at the very end, with encouragement for everyone to embrace and offer that peace to each person present; this would be a way of saying *good-bye* (which literally is a contraction of "God be with you").

4:15 End.

CONTINUING GROUPS

What do we need to pay attention to in a group that is made up of people who have completed an introductory group? In answering this, we need to keep in mind that this group may not be comprised of the same people who were together before. Shalem has several continuing groups, each made up of people from a number of different introductory groups. There are three requirements for entry: completion of an introductory group (this provides a certain shared understanding and experience); willingness to be committed for at least three months at a time, with the option of a nine-month commitment from the start; and a sense of personal need for the process of a continuing group as an aid for living in the Presence.

I say *process* rather than *content* advisedly, since we have found that what is most important to most people after introductory groups is not so much the specific new or repeated content as it is the process of attending God through all dimensions of our being in guided silence. Sharing becomes less important for many people after introductory groups, even a distraction for some. It is the disciplined, simple, collective silence, underlaid by a desire for God, that most steadily counts. This isn't to say that the content is irrelevant; it is just more clearly relativized to the shared Ground of all content which we find ourselves more directly and simply attending. Thus introductory words and sharing are often reduced, and the silence is extended.

Shalem has developed a loose four-year cycle of themes divided into three-month segments. These include the themes covered in part 1 of this book.[5] Each represents a particular dimension of life through which we can integrally attend God, self, and world. Most of these themes are introduced in introductory groups. We use the word *cycle* rather than *sequence* because the themes interpenetrate one another, and they do not form a gradation at the end of which one "graduates." After four years the cycle can begin again for those who want to continue, perhaps with some different emphases within the same theme areas.

Just as with the repetition of Sunday liturgies, what counts most is not new content, or an expectation of being "finished," but rather a continued offering of an environment for attending God directly, into which *we* bring the real newness: the ever-fresh vulnerability to the Spirit-at-work that grace shapes in us. Such groups, in comparison to formal liturgies, provide this opportunity with more precise emphasis on the interior noticing than on the exterior communalizing. The communalizing is inherently there in the groups also, though, since at our authentic interior center we are not cut off from others, rather, everyone (and everything) appears together.

Continuing groups provide opportunity to attend God and life more deeply through particular themes. This process can be assisted by a great many possible methods, a few of which are suggested in part 1 of this book. Just as in introductory groups, however, too many new methods can tempt distraction and fascination with the new. New methods can provide a helpful jolt and fresh perspective at times, but the key question to bring to prayer in discerning whether or not to use particular new or old methods is always the same: do they invite our spacious presence to God rather than constrictive presence to self? Sometimes a group can answer this best by simply repeating the same methods for long periods of time, or by just providing methodless silence.

Attendance in continuing long-term groups can be a little more sporadic than in introductory groups. People feel less compelled to always be present. As long as absences are not too frequent, this behavior is not nearly so disruptive as in introductory groups (though every absence affects the "flavor" of the group's shared experience to some extent). Most people have caught on by now to the fact that it is not grasping the content that counts, but opening to God through whatever is offered in the groups. Thus, people come a little more relaxed about the content and the group as a whole, not expecting any great end-all miracle or insight, but rather feeling committed to a more steady, long-haul, trusting evolution into God's pervasive yet elusive grace.

LOCAL CHURCH SETTING

If an introductory or continuing group is growing out of a local church's life, then it is important to keep it connected with the larger life of that church. Intensive groups in such settings may have the problem of being perceived by those not in them as elitist, self focused, potentially divisive, or not relevant to the "mainstream" of the local church's life. The reality at best is just the opposite: the group gives its members an environment to discover their deeper interdependence, unity, and mission with others in God, and in the process to find themselves in God's "mainstream." (Indeed, this is one way of seeing the primary purpose of the local church.) This awareness in turn can provide a more discerning eye for what one personally, and the local church, more generally, may be called to be and do. Group members thus can become fresh leaven for the church in its decision-making and activities, joining the leaven of others in the congregation whose graced eye is being developed through other means than the group's.

One small but significant influence that group members can have who belong to various committees and councils of the church is in the realm of prayer, not only on their own time, but in the church meetings themselves. For example, one might suggest that brief periods of prayerful silence be kept in meetings before important decisions are made (other suggestions for meetings are elaborated in chapter 7, "Acting"). My basic point here is simply to suggest that what happens in groups needs to seep helpfully into the life of the local church, as well as beyond in family, work, and community life.

It can be helpful to reflect together on the implications of the group for these various dimensions of living at a point late in the group's life. This is one way to help keep the group consciously connected with the larger life of God in the world. However, this should not be prematurely addressed or forced. Group members first need to just relax into their prayer and let their further conversion proceed as they are ready and graced. The larger connections will gradually emerge naturally out of this deepening life in God.

CHAPTER 11

Leadership and Its Development

What kind of leader is needed for such a spiritual formation group? I have saved this question for last, with the hope that all that has been said thus far would help with the answer. The most important qualification of all I believe is the realization that the ultimate leader of the group is God's Holy Spirit blowing through us. Since this Spirit is a mystery whose direction we cannot know ahead of time (John 3:8), we are left with the need for a leader who does not "take over" in some controlling way, as though she or he knows just what should happen and how to get it to happen. Rather, the need is for someone who can assist the creation of an environment in which everyone can relax their temptation to take over the time with their possessive egos, and instead become open to the One whose presence we realize through our simple trust.

A good group leader knows that such trust is fundamental. He or she can provide some water to nourish the trust. But it is the Spirit that gives the growth, and does so in a myriad of mysterious ways that leave us in awe. In this sense the leader's role is a very humble and delicate one: assisting an atmosphere that frees everyone to listen in simple trust to the Holy Wind blowing out our constricting scales and inspiring our spirits with fresh Presence, never being able to predict the forms this might take with particular people at particular times.

The leader also is one who encourages patient acceptance in those whose constrictions are dominating at this time despite their conscious willingness to release them, trusting that in God's own time all will be well. Such patience also is encouraged with people whose inner life is full of fireworks: images, voices, waves of powerful feelings, or the like. The leader can suggest that they not become too fearful or fascinated with any of these, but just accept them as part of the long-term, mysterious cleansing and conversion process going forward. In other words, the leader needs to be able to retain a certain alert, steady trust in turning to God through whatever is happening with people and to gently encourage this with others.

Such trust and turning requires regular practice in the leader's own life outside the group. It is essential for leaders to maintain their own daily unambiguous prayer time, and to turn to God through the activities of the day. And, though not essential, it could be very helpful to have a regular spiritual friend with whom to be accountable for attending the Spirit's interior movements, and/or some other intentional reflective process, such as a small group or journal keeping.

On the more technical side, certain gifts are helpful, including:[1]

1. A calm, confidence-evoking, caring personal presence exteriorly, matched interiorly by a confidence in God rather than in any capacity our willful egos may suppose exists apart from God.

2. A capacity to "sense" the group as a whole, noticing signs of restlessness, boredom, tiredness, anxiety, still attentiveness, confusion, etc. Such sensitivity can help the leader to lead accordingly: with more or less silence, shorter or longer talks, shifts in method, encouragement, and so forth.

3. A capacity to help provide an open environment for firsthand personal presence to God, as opposed to filling the time with conceptual content or interpretation that in effect takes the place of that firsthand presence. Any content is meant to help lead into that presence, not to be a substitute for it. Among other things this means the capacity to talk succinctly and also selectively, that is, saying only what will help people stay close to their immediate awareness of God's spacious presence. Further, though the environmental process and sometimes appropriate questioning and commenting can be in the leader's hands, the responsibility for interpretation of people's experience should remain with them, not with the leader or anyone else. Such an attitude respects the unique mystery of a person's unfolding in God.

More general theologizing, psychologizing, historicizing, story telling, or explaining that does not aim at a more direct presence to God's presence normally needs to be withheld in such a group unless it is done at a separate time where it will not distract from the needed opportunity for unambiguous direct attention to God. The most essential presentation the leader needs to be capable of is simple, clear instructions for particular prayer forms that can help a person's presence to God. This capacity includes a background of personal experience with the methods offered.

4. A willingness to sacrifice one's own fully relaxed contemplative presence for the sake of the group. In other words, a willingness to continually be in touch with the spiritual atmosphere of the group, helping to cultivate an environment in which participants are more free to relax into God. This includes everything from appropriate timekeeping, to careful presentation and selection of methods and com-

ments, to praying for individual members in their unique situations. The leader needs to be turning to God constantly in the name of the group, asking for God's will to be done. Ideally all this can happen out of a personal contemplative presence retained throughout the session. Practically, though, this is not often possible in its fullness for the average leader. Hopefully the leader will have another group or place where he or she can be more simply present to God as an end in itself.

5. A willingness to receive feedback about how well the above leadership functions are being carried out through such means as the midterm and final evaluations previously mentioned and through one's own prayerful discernment alone and possibly with a spiritual friend.

6. A humble recognition of the limits of one's understanding: not trying to say or do more than we really know or God is really inviting. This includes a recognition of the limits of our psychological knowledge, and the possible need to refer people for professional help in the rare event they become overwhelmed by some negative, destructive emotion in the group.

One of the best combination of leaders in Shalem's experience is a man and woman teamed together. This is particularly helpful if a group consists of both men and women, or if one wants to attract a mixed membership. We have found that it is usually more difficult for men than for women to join such a group (see chapter 5, "Communing," for discussion of men's and women's spirituality). The cultivation of men and women teams perhaps can model the rightness and potentially equal ease of such contemplative formation for both sexes.

Two leaders together (whether a man and woman or of the same sex) have the added advantage of relieving the weight of leadership for one another, and of being able to give each other regular feedback on their way of leading. For the group, the inevitably different styles, strengths, and insights of each person can prove complementarity and broadening.

THE DEVELOPMENT OF LEADERS

Potential leaders can easily be intimidated by the list of gifts, or qualifications for the role. Such anxiety can be lessened if we aim our confidence at God rather than ourselves. God can do great things through weak vessels. Only God finally is capable of leading such a group. When we realize this, we can go ahead and respond to the vague sense of calling we may have, and its confirmation through the encouragement of others. The less experience we have, the more we can restrict our role to a simple facilitation of the process and descriptive introductions of prayer methods. Sometimes this kind of leadership can be shared with others in a group, particularly if others have more experience with certain prayer forms. However, too much shifting of leadership can be disruptive to a group's simple interior presence.

The best kind of leadership preparation involves experience as a participant in such a group led by an experienced and credible facilitator, followed by a supervised apprenticeship with such a person, or in a special group leaders' program that includes such supervision. Shalem has been involved in special projects for the identification and preparation of such potentially gifted group leaders in selected local churches and now has developed a major program for such leaders working in any religious setting. I am convinced that a few such potentially gifted group leaders exist in most normal religious settings. Such people might find each other and join together for a common preparation process, through Shalem or otherwise.

It should not be discouraging that an ideal preparation is not available in many places. If we feel a call to such spiritual formation leadership, confirmed by others, and we are in a ripe setting for the foundation of such a group, then by all means we should jump in the best way we can. One purpose of this book is to give people in this situation some confidence and clarity of intent and method with which to begin.

We can begin very simply and humbly, minimizing our role as leader, while at the same time being bold enough to provide the minimal facilitation that people need. We can select methods out of this book or elsewhere (including our own modifications as these seem called for), always remembering to subordinate any method to the intent of directly attending God's presence. These methods can be provided using the basic rhythm and procedure for a group elaborated earlier, leaving the rest in God's hands. If people come ready to be vulnerable to God's life in them and the world, if they desire more than fear God's call to deepening liberation, intimacy, and compassion, then we can trust that grace will abound, despite and through our sometimes fumbling and groping ways as facilitator.

Appendix

SAMPLE GROUP EVALUATIONS (FOR GROUP LEADERS)

Note: These introductory group evaluations, as well as the continuing group one that follows, are strictly suggestive. They have evolved from Shalem groups over the years and no doubt will continue to evolve. Thus a group leader wishing to include such a written or oral evaluation can pick and choose among these suggestions, modify them, or use them as stimulus for developing her or his own evaluation. Participants normally should be asked to include their names.

MIDTERM EVALUATION

Your answers to these questions hopefully will help you clarify a little more where you are at this point, and also help your leader to be more sensitive to your own and others' situations and needs in the group.

1. What word(s) or images(s) come to mind when you think of your present state of spiritual awareness? ("My spiritual awareness now is like . . .")
2. What has been happening to you in recent months that leads to these word(s) or image(s)?
3. How does God seem most alive for you now? (Answer in a word or phrase: "God is . . .")
4. How does this divine aliveness seem to affect your sense of who you are?
5. How does your sense of God and self now seem to be affecting your relations with others?
6. What obstacles and confusions appear most disturbing at this point (if any)?
7. What seems to be most promising now in lightening these obstacles? (Examples: daily meditation/prayer/exercise, the arts, reading, sharing experiences with a friend or spiritual director,

works of compassion, attention to your vocational life, trusting God's acceptance of where you are, etc.)

8. Looking back, what has been most memorable and important to you in the group's life thus far (however painful or joyful)?

9. When we break up into small groups, (a) what has been most helpful for your attentiveness to and reflection on God, e.g., have the guiding questions given before the small group been personally and/or collectively helpful? Have the dynamics of the small group itself been helpful? (b) what seems to have gotten in the way of the small group being more helpful? Is there something you would like to see being done differently in the small group when we start up again?

10. Please comment on any change or emphasis you would like to see in content, format, or leadership style during the months ahead, including any particular feedback you would like to give particular leaders.

11. Please share any other comments you would like to make about the group or your own needs or gifts.

II. INTRODUCTORY GROUP FINAL EVALUATION

We have approached spiritual awareness through the following lenses. Please mark each in terms of its helpfulness to your presence for God from (7)-highest to (1)-lowest. Any short comments you would like to include, which might help us better present these lenses, would be appreciated.

____ Preliminary physical exercises and reflection on body prayer

____ Sound and chant

____ Sound (being behind it, not labeling it, sound and silence, etc.)

____ Scriptural meditation I: Psalm 139

____ Scriptural meditation II: Mark 10:46-52 (Bartimaeus)

____ Scriptural "homework" phrases

____ External foci: icons

____ Releasing our self-images ("Who am I?") in pairs: one another as icon

____ Interior focus: white light, as still (week 1), and as expanding (week 2)

____ Centering Prayer

____ Thoughts; space between thoughts; the internal observer

____ Releasing self to God through feelings; in pairs

____ Seeing through the mirror

____ Movement meditation ("going without leaving home")

____ Attention to our vocation (callings) now: to particular forms of spiritual discipline and to particular ministries

____ Journal keeping

____ Input by leaders on attitudes and approaches to spiritual development

____ Small group time

____ Plenary reflection time: hearing from each other

____ Silence

____ Group support (explicit or implicit) for your daily living/praying/awareness/caring

____ Other personal discipline separate from the group but influenced by it (e.g., maintaining a regular prayer discipline)

____ Initial and concluding written work (such as spiritual biography, "picture" of reality, "what my spiritual journey seems to be . . .," etc.)

Looking Back Over the Five Months.

1. What has been most important to you about the group?

2. Which method most "stuck" with you as a way of personal spiritual opening/attention to God?

3. What changes have you noticed (if any) that the group (or the Holy Spirit through the group) has influenced in terms of your *attitudes* (ways you see/approach life) and/or *behavior* (what you do with your energy, time, money, etc.) toward:
   a. yourself (including your sense of vocation)
   b. others (family, friends, workmates, strangers)
   c. God (including God in Christ)
   d. the Bible and Christian tradition (and other traditions)
   e. congregational (parish) life, worship, and aims
   f. work, social service, and justice concerns
   g. nature
   h. anything else

4. How would you have liked the group to be different? (i.e., what do you wish had been included, changed, or left out in terms of basic content, time structure, leadership, size and mix, standards, etc, of the group, not mentioned already in this evaluation or in your midterm evaluation?)

Questions 5, 6, and 7 are important to answer yourself; you may or may not want to share them with the leaders in writing here.

5. Where is the most important graced openness and clarity in your life now for which you give thanks?

6. Where do you sense is the most important remaining closedness and cloudiness in your life now that awaits the Spirit's opening and your responsiveness?

7. What use of your energies will best serve your "holy sanity" in the months ahead?

8. Any other comments:

III. BRIEF EVALUATION FOR A CONTINUING OR INTRODUCTORY GROUP

Note to group leaders: The following questions have been used with groups that have continued after an introductory group. They may be used as periodical checks every few months, or at the end of a year. They also could be used as part or all of a brief evaluation for introductory groups.

1. When I reflect back over these (months), what has most helped me be present to God in the group's content, process, and leadership?
2. What has interfered with this presence?
3. As I look ahead to the continuation of this group, what I sense will be most valuable to me here is:

Notes

INTRODUCTION

1. A favorite saying of the Colorado-based Spiritual Life Institute in its magazine, *The Desert Call*.
2. Gerald May, *Pilgrimage Home* (New York: Paulist Press, 1979), and Tilden Edwards, *Spiritual Friend* (New York: Paulist Press, 1980).
3. Sometimes this development flows in reverse: from a realized identity in God to an awareness of unity with creation.
4. In the natural contemplative awareness described, this dissolution of self-image and God-image also occurs. Thus the psychological phenomenon of natural (or *generally* graced, if we want to avoid inferring any ultimate separation of nature and grace), and more specifically graced contemplative awareness share these ingredients. The difference can be found both in the spiritual conditioning we bring *into* the awareness (e.g., how open and willing we are for God), and what comes *out* of the awareness (e.g., particular fruits of the Spirit (Gal. 5:22), indications of God directly at work in deepening our conversion).
5. James Finley, *Merton's Palace of Nowhere: A Search for God through Awareness of the True Self* (Notre Dame: Ave Maria Press, 1978), 134.
6. Ibid. This is a fine summary of Merton's lifetime struggle to understand the true and false self in relation to God, including references to Merton's major writings on this subject. See also Gerald May, *Will and Spirit: A Contemplative Psychology* (San Francisco: Harper & Row 1982). Refer especially to his discussions of self-image and self-definition which provide the most precise description I know of our different dimensions of self. *The Collected Works of St. John of the Cross*, (Washington, DC: Institute of Carmelite Studies Publications, 1973). This can be hard reading, but it probably represents the most thorough Christian description of the experienced human-divine relationship at its deeper levels; John's understanding is presented (together with some other mystics) in Francis Nemeck and Theresa Coombs, *The Spiritual Journey* (Wilmington: Michael Glazier, 1987). Beatrice Bruteau, "Prayer and Identity," *Contemplative Review* 16, no. 3 (Fall 1983). This includes a lucid description of the different levels of Jesus' (and our) identity, reflected in his different ways of praying. For a historical view, see Ken Wilber, *Up From Eden* (Boston: New Science Library, 1986).

CHAPTER 1: GROUNDING

1. See chapter 7 (page 99) for a discussion of the process of discernment.
2. For those unfamiliar with prayer language in different traditions, it might be worth

pointing out here that *meditation* in classical Christian prayer normally has referred to some kind of active prayer, a dwelling on some particular word, image, or feeling in relation to God. *Contemplation*, on the other hand, normally refers to attention to God more directly, through and beyond any words, images, or feelings. This understanding is confused by the frequent use of the word *meditation* to refer to certain Eastern religious forms of contemplation. It is further confused by the use of the word *contemplation* to include *meditation* in Ignatian (Jesuit) tradition.

3. I am indebted to my colleague Gerald May for this insight.
4. Many early Greek Fathers speak of prayer as a function of the heart. See Kallistos Ware, "Ways of Prayer and Contemplation," *Christian Spirituality: Origins to the Twelfth Century*, ed. Bernard McGinn et al. (New York: Crossroad, 1985).
5. St. Seraphim of Sarov, *Little Russian Philokalia* (Platina, Calif.: St. Herman of Alaska Brotherhood, 1980), 1:49.
6. Moving from the image to the likeness of God is a favorite description of the spiritual journey in the writings of the early Greek Fathers. For a summary description, see Leonid Ouspensky and Vladimir Lossky, *The Meaning of Icons* (Crestwood, N.Y.: St. Vladimir's Press, 1982), 34.

CHAPTER 2: EMBODIMENT

1. See J. A. T. Robinson, *The Body: A Study in Pauline Theology* (Naperville, Ill.: Alec Allenson, 1957).
2. Pride, covetousness, lust, envy, gluttony, anger, sloth (accidie).
3. From the *Philokalia*, quoted by Ouspensky, *Meaning of Icons* (NY: SVS Press, 1982), 39.
4. Secondary mystical and charismatic phenomena (e.g., ecstasy and rapture, visions, locutions) can be seen as forms of participation in this integral Body. As Harvey Egan, S. J., says, "Not only the person's spirit, but also his psychosomatic structure, can and should anticipate in some way the glory of the beatific vision and life in the risen body," *Christian Mysticism* (Pueblo, Colo.: Pueblo Publishing Co., 1984), 336. See 304-336 for a description of these phenomena.
5. For a scholarly analysis of the body as viewed by Christian writers in the first Christian millennium, see Margaret Miles, *Fullness of Life* (Philadelphia: Westminster, 1982).
6. Roughly 7½" high in front, slanted up to 8½" in back, with a seat measuring 7" × 16" or more.
7. Tilden Edwards, *Living Simply Through the Day*, (New York: Paulist Press, 1977), 58-71.
8. Tarthang Tulku, *Kum Nye Relaxation*, 2 vols. Emeryville, Calif.: Dharma Publishing, 1978).
9. *The Complete Poems of Emily Dickinson*, ed. Thomas Johnson (Boston: Little, Brown & Co. 1957).
10. This is my own adaptation and Christian interpretation of an exercise I was taught many years ago by the Tibetan lama, Tarthang Tulku. His original version is printed in *Time, Space, and Knowledge* (Emeryville, Calif.: Dharma Publishing, 1977), 185. For an alternative, see Nhat Hanh, *A Guide to Walking Meditation* (Nyack, N.Y.: Fellowship of Reconciliation, 1985).
11. Found in a paper presented at the Institute for Spirituality, St. John's University, Collegeville, Minn., 1978.
12. Elmer O'Brien, ed., *Varieties of Mystical Experience* (New York: Holt, Rinehart & Winston, 1964), 98.
13. A good general book on the history and practice of fasting in Christian tradition is Thomas Ryan, *Fasting Rediscovered* (New York: Paulist Press, 1981).
14. One relevant recipe book is Virgina Richardson, *Feasts for Feast Days* (New York: The Episcopalian, 1985).
15. Quoted in Ryan, *Fasting Rediscovered*, 27.

CHAPTER 3: SOUND AND SILENCE

1. For the Jesus Prayer, see Timothy Ware, ed., *The Art of Prayer* (London: Faber & Faber, 1966); and R. M. French, trans., *The Way of a Pilgrim* (San Francisco: Harper & Row/Seabury Press, 1965). For an example of a related contemporary form, see John Main, O.S.B., *Word into Silence* (New York: Paulist Press, 1981).
2. The most practical guide to Centering Prayer I have found is Thomas Keating, *Open Mind, Open Heart* (Warwick, N.Y.: Amity House, 1986). Also see Keating, Basil Pennington, and Thomas Clarke, *Finding Grace at the Center* (Still River, Mass.: St. Bede Publishers, 1978), and Pennington's *Centering Prayer* (New York: Image, 1982). A cassette tape on Centering Prayer by Pennington is available from Credence Cassettes, a service of the National Catholic Reporter Publishing Co., P.O. Box 414291, Kansas City, Mo 64141.

CHAPTER 4: SEEING

1. Kena Upanishads (1:1); Matt. 13:16.
2. See Tilden Edwards, *Sabbath Time* (New York: Seabury Press, 1982), 31-32, including references to the research of Robert Bellah.
3. Matthew Fox, ed., *Meditations with Meister Eckhart* (Santa Fe: Bear & Co., 1982), 21.
4. See Margaret Miles, *Image as Insight* (Boston: Beacon Press, 1985), especially chapters 5,6,7. She offers seminal historical and contemporary insights on the place of religious images in forming the spiritual heart.
5. Ouspensky and Lossky, *Meaning of Icons*, 40-41. I am particularly indebted to Ouspensky's description of iconographic history and theology for much of my best theoretical knowledge of icons. The book also has a wonderful collection of icons, in color, carefully interpreted. Another more comprehensive introduction to icons is John Baggley, *Doors of Perception* (Crestwood, NY: St. Vladimir's Seminary Press, 1988).
6. Ibid., 30.
7. Ibid., 44.
8. See ibid., 48, for the causes and forms of this distortion.
9. For a personal and spiritual interpretation of this icon, see Henri Nouwen, *Behold the Beauty of the Lord* (Notre Dame: Ave Maria Press, 1987). Excellent wood-mounted reproductions in varying sizes can be ordered from Printery House, Conception, Mo 64433.
10. See May, *Will and Spirit*. Thomas Merton, "The Inner Experience," *Cistercian Studies*, vol. 18, no. 1 (Winter 1983) and installments in succeeding issues. I am particularly indebted to the oral instruction I have received from Tarthang Tulku that I have adapted over the years for use in contemplative spiritual formation in a Christian context. His influence is particularly seen in parts of exercises 4, 7, 8 and 9. See some of his relevant books: *Gesture of Balance* (1977); *Openness Mind* (1978); *Reflections of Mind* (1975); and *Knowledge of Freedom* (1984), all published by Dharma Publications, Emeryville, Calif.

CHAPTER 5: COMMUNING

1. This "everything" includes a mutual belonging of time, space, and knowledge in a way that is far more coinherent and immediately present than our "outside" minds perceive. See Tulku's explanation and revealing set of experiential exercises in his *Time, Space, and Knowledge* (Emeryville, CA: Dharma Pubs. 1977) and its sequels.
2. Ibid., part 1. For more precise and extensive exercises that can help you go further with such meditation on the body, I recommend the relevant exercises in this book. You can make your own transposition into a Christian or other context.
3. For other perspectives on sexuality and spirituality, see May, *Will and Spirit*, pp. 149-

60, 189-94; Ann and Barry Ulanov, *Primary Speech* (Atlanta: John Knox Press, 1982), chapter 8.

4. Ibid. See section on "Knowledge" for one way of understanding and experiencing this intrinsic knowing quality.

5. Among many fine books on family spirituality I would especially recommend Dolores Leckey, *The Ordinary Way* (New York: Crossroad, 1982).

6. See Edwards, *Sabbath Time*, especially part 4.

7. Sandra Schneiders, "Effects of Women's Experience on Spirituality," *Women's Spirituality*, ed. Joann Wolski Conn (New York: Paulist Press, 1986), 42. According to Schneiders, this sense of end-in-itself relationship with God can be crippled for women if they have absorbed a sense of God as a masculine judge of intrinsically unworthy women, leading to guilt and a compensatory focus on self-effacing service and performance.

8. See John Fortunato, *Embracing the Exile* (New York: Seabury Press, 1982) for a poignant sense of homosexual spiritual and psychological experience.

9. This is a blunt phrase of Parker Palmer used in a workshop on solitude and community at Shalem in 1985. He plans to develop this into a book. Dr. Palmer has a long background with intentional Christian communities, and my own intuitions have developed further confidence, clarity, and enrichment from him.

10. See Edwards, *Sabbath Time*, part 4, for concrete suggestions.

11. Edwards, *Sabbath Time*, ch. 8; *All God's Children* (Nashville: Abingdon Press, 1982), ch. 5. For further material on liturgical spirituality, see *Studies in Formative Spirituality* 3, no. 3 (Nov. 1982).

CHAPTER 6: RE-MEMBERING

1. The most precise description of such "great time" I have found, together with exercises to aid its understanding, is found in Tulku, *Time, Space, and Knowledge*, part 2.

2. I know of no significant contemplative writings specifically on healing. For a general and practical history of healing ministry in the Church, see Francis MacNutt, *Healing* (New York: Bantam, 1980). See also the books of Matthew and Dennis Linn, e.g., *Healing of Memories* (Notre Dame: Ave Maria Press, 1977).

3. See the appendix in Tolbert McCarroll, *Guiding God's Children* (New York: Paulist Press, 1983), for a practical way of using haiku in a spiritual context. The haiku by Ken Feit is used with permission of Bear and Co., Inc., Santa Fe, N.M.

4. Since presence for God is the key intent of prayer, we need to remember that whatever frees that presence is the kind of prayer called for at a given time. This may come in our preparatory prayer even before beginning to read Scripture, or it may come through the "scripture of our life" in some particular way apart from direct Bible reading. Scripture is a priviledged resource for prayer, but God appears to us in manifold ways. Thus we need not cling to Scripture if in fact some other avenue is taking us to that living presence at a given time.

5. Quoted in Chester Michael and Marie Norrisey, *Prayer and Temperament* (Charlottesville, Va.: The Open Door) 32. A more detailed description of *lectio divina* is given here also. For further explanation, see Basil Pennington's chapter on it in *Living with Apocalypse* (San Francisco: Harper & Row, 1984).

6. The longest version of the historical Jesus Prayer that rose among the Desert Fathers and Mothers is, "Lord Jesus Christ have mercy on me, a sinner". It has often shortened, for example, to "Lord Jesus Christ have mercy on me". See chapter 3, note 1, for several reading references.

7. John Veltri, *Orientations* (Guelph, Ontario: Loyola House, 1979), 1:25.

CHAPTER 7: ACTING

1. Quoted in R. Restak, *The Brain* (New York: Bantam, 1984), 136. My colleague Gerald May is involved in reviews of the explosive new knowledge of the human brain as it relates to our spiritual nature and development.
2. Ralph Burhoe, from an article in the *National Catholic Reporter* (5 September 1980).
3. See 2 Cor. 11:14.
4. I would especially recommend Thomas Green, *Weeds Among the Wheat* (Notre Dame: Ave Maria Press, 1984). See also May, *Will and Spirit*, 287-290, for its psychological and contemplative context and a footnoted bibliography.
5. See the discussion of this in David Lonsdale, "Traditions of Spiritual Guidance: *The Cloud of Unknowing*," *The Way* 26, no. 2 (April 1986): 158.
6. I am indebted to Green, *Weeds Among the Wheat*, for this insight.
7. I am indebted to my colleague Sister Rose Mary Dougherty for her personal insights concerning discernment, as well as Scripture.
8. See Edwards, *Spiritual Friend*, for help in understanding the nature of spiritual friendship.
9 See Edwards, *Sabbath Time*, for a detailed understanding of this rhythm of time.
10. Ivan Illich, quoted in the *Utne Reader* (April-May 1985) 73-74, from an article in *Church World* by Susan Hunt, "Ivan Illich: Economic Agnostic."
11. For some of these insights I am indebted to Raimundo Pannikar and his interpretation in a lecture by my colleague Dolores Leckey. See his article in *Cross Currents* (Fall 1981). Another helpful document related to work is Pope John Paul II, *The Encyclical on Human Work* (Washington, DC: Office of Publication, U.S. Catholic Conference, 1981), which is broadly applicable on an ecumenical basis.
12. An excellent Quaker history and description of their ways of conducting meetings for business is found in Michael Sheeran, *Beyond Majority Rule* (Philadelphia Yearly Meeting of the Religious Society of Friends, 1985).
13. Meister Eckhart adds his own twist: "To Live the wayless way, free and yet bound to live *among* things but not *in* things. All God's friends live this way . . . among cares but not within cares." Fox, ed., *Meditations with Meister Eckhart*, 115.
14. For an excellent biblical and theological exposition concerning money, see John Haughey, *The Holy Use of Money* (Garden City, N.Y.: Doubleday, 1986), especially chapter 1.
15. Keating, *Open Mind, Open Heart*.
16. Ram Dass and Paul Gorman, *How Can I Help? Stories and Reflections On Service* (New York: Alfred A. Knopf, 1985).
17. Beatrice Bruteau, "Insight and Manifestation: A Way of Prayer in Christian Context," *Contemplative Review* 16, no. 3 (Fall 1983): 20.

CHAPTER 8: APPRECIATING

1. "The Living Flame of Love," *The Collected Works of St. John of the Cross*, 584.
2. See Edwards, *Sabbath Time*, chapters 7 and 8.
3. For further understanding of Eucharist as a school prayer, see Robert Duggan, "Liturgy and Spirituality," *Spiritual Life* 27, no. 1 (Spring 1981). See also the whole issue of *Studies in Formative Spirituality* 3, no. 3 (November 1982).
4. "The Spiritual Espousals" in *John Ruusbroec* trans. James Wiseman (New York: Paulist Press, 1985), 80.
5. Quoted in A. M. Allchin, *The Living Presence of the Past* (New York: Seabury Press, 1981), 91.
6. Julian of Norwich, recording Jesus' "showing" to her. See her *Showings* trans. E. Colledge and J. Walsh (New York: Paulist Press, 1978).

CHAPTER 9: INTENT AND METHOD

1. May, *Pilgrimage Home.*
2. See Edwards, *Spiritual Friend*, ch. 7.
3. Isaac Penington, *Works*, (Sherwood, N.Y.: David Heaton, 1863), 4:55, as quoted in *Quaker Spirituality*, ed. Douglas Steere (New York: Paulist Press, 1984), 28.

CHAPTER 10: RHYTHM

1. David Hay, *Exploring Inner Space* (New York: Penguin, 1982), 114 ff.
2. Shalem's introductory and continuing groups have ranged in size from ten to thirty members.
3. A more elaborate process of questioning that has been developed and used from time to time in Shalem groups is summarized in "The Self-Search Format", in May, *Pilgrimage Home*, 117-128.
4. Ibid., 105, for an earlier version of these.
5. The themes have been rearranged in this book, with a number conflated together in some chapters. "Historical holiness" is the one theme not present here. This would include attention to great contemplative writings, perhaps including personal journal dialogues with some of their authors.

   There is nothing sacred about this particular way of making distinctions in the spiritual life, since all its dimensions are so intertwined. It could just as easily be divided and labeled in many other ways. Here is the list of the twelve themes: understanding our spiritual nature (grounding); embodiment (body prayer); listening and voicing; Scripture as icon; seeing; questioning the mind; re-membering; communing; acting; appreciating; historical holiness.

CHAPTER 11: LEADERSHIP AND ITS DEVELOPMENT

1. This list of gifts elaborates or complements those mentioned in my book, *Spiritual Friend*, 188-192. Further discussion of leadership can be found in May, *Pilgrimage Home*, 17-23.